T0196905

Other books by Celine Koropchak

One With All of Thee: Growing Your Sacred Connection

One With All of Thee:
Sowing the Seeds For Change

Divine Writings from
The Tovarysh Connection
VOLUME TWO IN THE OWAT SERIES

Celine Koropchak

BALBOA.
PRESS
A DIVISION OF HAY HOUSE

Balboa Press books may be ordered through booksellers or by contacting:

Balboa Press
A Division of Hay House
1663 Liberty Drive
Bloomington, IN 47403
www.balboapress.com
1 (877) 407-4847

Print information available on the last page.

ISBN: 978-1-5043-8487-2 (sc)
ISBN: 978-1-5043-8488-9 (hc)
ISBN: 978-1-5043-8489-6 (e)

Library of Congress Control Number: 2017911825

Balboa Press rev. date: 09/25/2017

To Nina, Alice, Jeanne, Sharon and Terry

I could not have done it without you

Contents

Note to Readers

We have all noticed the changes on this planet, from those by Mother Nature to the rise of a fearful atmosphere created by her charges. These are all a part of the growth of the cosmic consciousness, as the universal shift continues to occur.

As the messages of this book offer to you a guidepost to find your own way forward, you will undoubtedly go through your own personal changes. Some might be very subtle, while others may be more distinct and profound. Whichever personal changes begin to appear in your life, embrace them with the knowledge that their appearance is an indicator of your own personal growth.

As you become aware of these personal changes, I encourage you not to be fearful of them. Reading these passages, as simple as they might seem, will reveal to you your own true nature. And slowly your energetic vibration will rise, allowing your personal guides to work more closely with you, as you become more receptive to the higher energies around you.

If you find increased sensitivities in any of your physical senses, allow that to unfold, and adjust your life to accommodate them. This might include clairaudience, clairvoyance or clairsentience. With the rising energies upon this planet, more people are discovering these gifts in themselves.

If you find yourself avoiding crowds, then accept that change and surround yourself with a white light of protection, or carry the appropriate stones to aid you when you are out in public.

If you find your physical body requires more rest, find the time to give it that rest. Honor this temple which houses your soul with nourishing food and plenty of water, and offer it love for getting you to this point in your life.

It is impossible for you to go through this alone. For truthfully, you are never alone, and your personal guides will be there for you at the moment you call to them. Do call on them, as they are so anxious to help and comfort you.

But finding others whom you trust to share this experience with will also be most helpful to you. These could be friends, spiritual teachers, spiritual groups or counselors, for personal growth includes working through those darker aspects of your life. By bringing these aspects out into the light and reflecting upon them, you will be better able to release them in forgiveness and love. There are many tools out there to help make this process as gentle as possible for you. Don't try to do this alone.

If you are reading this book, I suspect that you are searching, and I hope that you will find some direction from the pages here before you. But I do encourage you to question everything, be it writings from this book or from any other venue offering guidance. And if the teachings don't resonate with you, then put them aside and find another venue to help you on your search. For there are many paths to personal growth, and we are all at a different point on our own paths. There is a perfect one out there for you. Trust your intuition to show you the way.

I have been on this journey for a long time and feel there is still so very much for me to learn. Be gentle with yourself, and do not compare your progress with that of any other; for you are unique in what you have to learn and in the gift you have to share with the world.

Be creative, be of joy and be that being of light that you truly are! Shine your light on others and trust the synchronicities in your life to guide you on your journey.

And thank you, for allowing me the honor and the privilege of helping you find your way.

Preface

During my morning meditation today, as I asked for guidance on how to present this book to you, a guide who I haven't heard from in a few years came to visit. Whenever this gentle loving spirit comes through, I smile so much my mouth hurts. And her favorite word this morning was *wondrous*. How this earthly existence is a wondrous opportunity to experience life to the fullest.

As we move through this period of intense change, the message to me, and to all of us, was to view this world through the lens of wonder and love rather than the lens of fear. For change brings with it the possibility for growth, not only for this planet, but for the entirety of being.

It is so easy to want to stay with the status quo, in that place of comfort where we know exactly what we will do each day; to go through the motions of our lives automatically without really engaging. We as humans are resistant to change. For change brings with it an uncertainty about what the outcomes will be, should we choose that other path never before taken.

For over 25 years, I have received these messages from my guides, my Tovarysh, without sharing them, until I was finally asked to put them out into the world. My immediate response was one of fear. 'You want me to do *what?*' I've always been a private person, and the thought of going public with one of the most private parts of my life left me shaking in my boots. But I also understood that these messages needed to be shared, that they were no longer just for me.

So I took that unknown path, trusting the guidance I received… and my worst fears of being chastised and ridiculed never came to be. Instead, I was thanked by many for inspiring them with these words. I heard from many that these words helped them to walk through their own fears. And doors have begun to open for me that I never expected. I have been interviewed on BlogTalkRadio more than once. I have had the opportunity to speak to various groups and to teach about how to move through life without fear, empowering others to discover their own gifts to be shared. And the joy and satisfaction I have felt watching others blossom in front of my eyes... wondrous!! I continue to share my blog, *TheTovaryshConnection*, along with other pieces I've written in my own voice. That initial fear is gone, and although I still get nervous, I also feel that I am doing what I came here to do...share my gift with you.

I'm thrilled to be able to offer you a second book of messages during these turbulent times. The fact that this book has numerous passages on fear is timely, as fear seems to pervade our world these days. *'Sowing the Seeds for Change'* continues to build on the messages from the first book, with simple, yet powerful words to gently guide you forward on your path.

My hope is that this OWAT series will help you to accept the truth that you are a Divine being, on a journey of personal growth through the human experience. It begins with learning to love yourself and understanding that all of creation is Divine. Yes, even your greatest adversaries.

My hope is that by reading these messages, you will realize how we are all connected, allowing you to change your perception of life from one that is personal, to a higher perspective, one that is more universal. Your life is unfolding exactly as it should in the most perfect way. I truly believe this, as more is revealed to me each day. The intricate web of connection that I have begun to trust has allowed me to follow the synchronicities in my own life, for I know they are lovingly guiding me forward. And this loving view has changed my life, as it can change yours. Allow it to come from your heart, from your own Divinity, with your innate knowledge that love is all there is.

Come with me and share this journey of Divine inspiration. Accept this day and every day as a *wondrous* opportunity to experience life. Believe in yourself as I believe in you. And allow the seeds of change to sprout and empower you. Together, in loving connection, we CAN change the world.

Celine Koropchak
March 2017

Week 1

What of...Life?

You have been given the gift of life.
You are conscious of your surroundings.
You are sentient and have feelings.
You are able to think, to create,
To connect with other sentient beings.
And yet, how many of you are truly living?

How many of you are actually thinking, feeling, creating and connecting with others? How many of you are just going through the motions of daily living, like an automaton, as in one of your movies? Do you ever wonder why, how, who, when and what if?

Your current state of being is encased within a human form, for the most part...or at least that is how most of you relate to life. *I am a physical being with physical limitations, with physical vulnerabilities, with physical pain and suffering, in a physical form that ages daily, then takes its last breath, and that is the end of life as I know it.* Many believe that is the extent of it, of life...and then comes oblivion.

When, over this short course of time, are you going to *live* your life? Tomorrow? When you have more time, more money, more energy, or more freedom? What about now, in this very moment? Can you break free from the chains of complicity that have bound you so tightly, you do not even know how to move, to breathe, to dance?

Now, *this* moment, is the perfect time to begin your life. With no judgments, no regrets of past actions, no fear of future possibilities. You are living your life at this very moment...breathing in and out, in and out. And now the time is ripe for your dreams, your hopes, and your visions to manifest. The energy is rising. The group consciousness is stirring into action. The Universe, the entire Universe, is beginning to take a deep breath to release the ways of the past and to bring in your dreams of the future.

And what are those dreams of yours? Do they consist of fear, dread, worries and doubts? Do they immobilize you? Have they even managed to make it to the very surface of your consciousness? Or are they buried so deep within you, they are inaccessible to your conscious mind?

The Universe is listening to you! It is preparing to serve you the very thing that you have ordered from the menu. Be it joy and hope, or fear and dread. What does your palate crave today? You deserve only joy and love. And yet, you order less, much less than that for yourselves.

If you could change your world today, how would you change it?

Sit, breathe, close your eyes and see that world before you. Create the energy of that world in your mind's eye with love, only with love. Smile as you do this and allow the creativity to flow. Do it this very instant, exist in that world for a moment. Draw it to you and watch it unfold. Breathe life into it. For all creation requires the breath of life…and so, too, your creations require your breath of life.

Not only do you have the gift of life, you have the gift, the ability, of creating life around you. It is your choice to create that which you want. Will you be passive and live in others' creations, or will you create your own world in which to live?

Will you be passive in this physical existence and complacently go through your allotted time? Or will you be active and learn the steps to your dance, the dance of your spirit and your soul?

Can you hear the beat? Listen. It may be faint, but it is there. Listen and feel the beat of *your* song, *your* music; for the Universe sings to you every moment of your day. And it is time for you now to get up and dance. Open your arms and spin your world around you.

Accept the gift of this life with joy. And once you do, you will understand that your very existence is limitless. Neither time nor space can limit who you are, for your very being exists within the All.

For you *are* the All.

Week 2

What Comes Now?

Your seasons here upon this physical plane
Are now changing;
Some areas of the Mother
Are moving into a period of growth
While other areas are coming into a period of rest.
In synchronicity and yet in opposite directions.
Is that not the way of life here on this physical plane?
The give and take.
Of life. Of energy. Of joy. Of love.

Remember that all are connected, so what may be perceived as a loss from one viewing frame appears as a gain from the equal and opposite viewing frame. It is really neither, but just the movement of energy from one position to another. There really is never loss or gain, just movement and flow. That is how things really work in the Universe. However, you still do not seem to accept this concept within the physical realm.

This is partially due to the inability of many to recognize the connectedness of the All. They still believe that *more for you means less for me*. How is this possible when you are all One? External conflict truly becomes internal conflict, until one can understand the ways of the Universe.

As we continue the lessons of these writings, let this truth be known. All life is energy, including your thoughts, words and deeds. Energy cannot be created or destroyed. Therefore, it is in a constant state of transition or transformation. The words you speak are composed of energy that goes out into the ethers, to be accepted or rejected by another in the form of thoughts or deeds. Perhaps it is transformed to another's words with their energy and back into the ethers. It is cyclic, it is never-ending and it is all connected.

Knowing this, try to understand how everything works together, even though it may not appear that way at first viewing. Can you work *with* the perceived limitations that you have, rather than trying to will those limitations into something that they are not? It is a dance - the dance of life…and too many of you are trying to lead when not knowing the steps to the dance.

Understand that all is as it should be. And whether you can see it or not, there *is* forward movement. It may not appear that way from your perspective, because you have only a limited view in this physical realm. But remember that this is not the only plane of existence, and your actions here upon this physical plane are teaching others in different realms how to grow. Whatever is occurring in your life at this moment is not for naught. It has purpose. *You* have purpose and are a very important piece of the mosaic of life.

We cannot emphasize enough your connection to the All. Remember this before you speak or act, and give gratitude for what you have in your life. The concept of *haves and have-nots* does not make sense in a world where All are One. Remember that your lessons, your growth, your life contribute to the All. They have a purpose far greater than you are aware!

There are no small acts, no insignificant lives, and no worthless deeds. It is all greatness, all powerful and all with significant purpose. No matter what does or does not happen in your life, you have contributed to the growth of the All, the Universe. And that is no insignificant contribution.

You have our gratitude for what you have given us. And we shall continue to return to you all the love that you can hold, all the joy that you can accept and all the guidance for which you ask.

For we are one with you in love…always.

Week 3

Know No Fear

What of this emotion
That has been predominant in your life
For as far back as you can remember?
How does this emotion serve you?
And how does it serve the Universe
In its growth and expansion?

The simple answer is that it does not. It does not serve you or this physical world or the Universe. Yet it is prevalent everywhere you look. It has inculcated your very existence, to the extent that you do not even realize that it is a constant presence in your life.

And so, what of fear? What is this power over you and your world, such that fear is continuously invited into every thought, word and action on this physical plane? Can you step back for a moment and be an observer in your life, in order to see how powerful you have allowed this emotion to become?

There is the fear of aging, the fear of rejection, the fear of the unknown, the fear of lack, the fear of plenty, the fear of what just occurred, the fear of what did not occur. No matter what your situation, your status, your gender, or your age, there it is creeping into your conscious, your subconscious world. Why? Why do you allow this Ego-driven emotion to control how you live your days, your precious days here upon this plane?

For a moment, just for a moment, can you allow all that fear to fall from your immediate environment, as dirt washes from your physical body? Set down the weight of the burden of fear, and observe the lightness that you suddenly feel. Can you feel the edges of your mouth beginning to curl into a smile, a laugh, a song that affects your entire being? All because you released yourself from the shackles of fear, for just a moment. Imagine how the entire world would change if everyone did this exercise at the very same instant of time!

It is possible to release yourself from this burden, entirely possible. But first you must observe and note how much this emotion rules your life. Once you stop and take a good look, you will be astonished at what you see! The next step is to slowly replace that fear with love, for that is truly all there is. This cloud of fear shades the brilliant light that shines within and around each and every one of you. *Each* and *every one* of you!

Do not let fear hold you back any longer. Do not allow it to prevent you from unfolding your wings in preparation for taking flight…not to run, but to soar. Why do you settle for crawling around on your belly, when you can soar above it all? You do not realize the power that you have within you. So retrieve the power that you have given to fear. Take it back, replace it in its true form within you, and feel the change in your physical, emotional and mental beings!

The first step is to recognize the presence of fear. The second step is to replace that fear with love. And all the remaining steps of your forward movement will gently and quickly fall into place. Do not hold your breath! Blow out the fear. Reclaim your power and see how far you can fly!

And if that first step is tenuous, call upon us. We shall light the way until your own brilliance lights the path ahead of you. Ah, if you can only see the possibilities, the exquisite beams of light that shine within each and every one of you.

We shall be here beside you, until you no longer need our support. But until then, we shall always be here with a helping hand, an encouraging and gentle push forward.

Ah, what lies ahead is only brilliance and light!
Shine brightly as you were meant to do!

Week 4

What of...Ego?

What is this thing called Ego?
Does it have a place in your immediate world?
You have the terms for it...
That person has a big Ego, or is *egocentric* or *ego-driven*.
Does it have a purpose here for you
Or should you deny its very existence?

Ego is a constant presence on this physical plane, and it is supported by the feeling of separateness caused by your individual physical forms. Without these forms, it has no reason for being, as the Oneness of All is much easier to understand. But individual personality exists across all planes, to a greater or lesser degree, depending on the location. You are all a part of the Oneness, yet you are all individual spirits and souls with individual lessons or tasks to experience in your lives.

As you grow spiritually, becoming more aware of the Oneness, with better understanding of the Universal ways, you also realize that Ego is a part of your existence that is no longer necessary for you. However, as a child first coming into being on this plane, you rely on Ego to help you transition from the non-physical plane to the physical plane. If you did not have Ego present, you would not be able to best learn the lessons that precipitated your existence here on this plane in the first place. For if you understood the Oneness of Being throughout your entire life, many lessons would be moot and not necessary to learn.

The problem occurs when you become too accustomed to the way of Ego and fail to realize its intended purpose in your life. When

Ego continues to grow in strength, it begins to overshadow your connection to the Divine, thus making the connection to the All less apparent to you. Ego was never intended to overpower the Divine connection, as it has in so many of you. This makes your journey back into the loving embrace of the All a longer and often more challenging journey.

Allowing Ego to have a small presence in your life is most certainly acceptable and actually helpful, as you continue on your path to knowledge. It is when Ego blinds you with false illusions of grandeur that it becomes a burden for you, slowing down your forward movement.

Do not berate yourself for a flare of Ego as you live your daily life. But do become vigilant when it begins to overtake your thoughts, feeding itself by taking power away from others and encouraging you to forget the ways of kindness and compassion. That is when it is time to take a step back and ask yourself the question, 'Why?' *Why am I doing this? Why am I thinking this way? Why am I saying these things?*

Be aware of your thoughts, words and deeds every day, and how they may affect others who cross your path. If you find yourself making excuses for these thoughts, words or deeds, then begin to watch for the presence of Ego in your life. Perhaps it has overgrown its boundaries and needs to be pruned back to a smaller size.

And if ever you stumble or need a helping hand, know that we are always here beside you, basking in your light, awaiting the day of your return to your true state…when we shall welcome you home with love and gratitude.

> Do not allow Ego to shade the brilliant Divine light
> That shines from within you.
> Do not doubt for a moment the existence of this
> Divine light and the power of it.
> Do not forget your connection to the All.

Week 5

Thoughts

Have you ever had something come to mind
And within the next moment or few hours,
Exactly what you were thinking came to pass?
Perhaps you were thinking of a friend or loved one
And they called.
Perhaps you were wondering when
It was going to start raining
And the next moment it began.
Or perhaps, you mistakenly made
A wrong turn driving home
Avoiding an accident that occurred
On your usual route

Why do these things happen to you? Do you have an innate knowledge of what is going to happen? Have you the ability to manifest certain things to occur in your life? Or was it just a coincidence? What do you think? How do you explain it?

We have mentioned the web of connection to you before. All are connected by a web of energy, similar in concept to your internet. What occurs on one end of the web can be picked up on the opposite end at various time points, depending upon the speed of your connection. We know this is a good metaphor to explain what happens on an energetic level, because many are using that same type of connection to read these words.

Is it such a great leap then, to accept a web of connection at a higher frequency, that is not a part of this physical world, but more a part of the energetic plane? This physical body you currently inhabit is necessary for lessons to be learned here upon this plane. But it is not necessary for your existence in your natural state. And when you have experiences as have been described here, you have tapped into that energetic web that is constantly pulsing with messages, ideas, and knowledge.

This is possible for every one of you, without exception. The fact that the scribe of these messages is able to write is because she has allowed herself to be open to the energetic connections that abound in this physical world, just not in a fashion to which you are accustomed.

It is possible for every one of you to make a connection and find the way best to receive the knowledge available to you. It is just a matter of quieting your mind, of trusting your own abilities and approaching this means of communication with love and not fear. If what you hear is not of light and love, then it is not from us or from the web of love that surrounds each and every one of you. And should that occur, call on us immediately to surround you with love and light.

Remember that you are a Divine being who inhabits a physical body to learn lessons for the group consciousness, for that web of connection. This means that any piece of information that has been received through that web is available to you. What we are trying to say is that the information, the knowledge which you seek, comes from within, not from without. For this web of connection flows from Divine light to Divine light to Divine light; and your inner core *is* that Divine light.

When these thoughts come to you, do not shake your head in disbelief and fear. Instead give gratitude that you have experienced a very natural phenomenon that occurs constantly. You may just need more time, more practice, to accept the gift of these thoughts, this connection.

The energies of this physical plane are rising, which means that these connections will become stronger and be made more frequently between all of those connected to the energetic web. Accept these connections. And if you have questions, still your mind and give yourself time to sit quietly. Then call upon us to help you find clarity.

You hold the power of the connection in your hands. Use it gently. Use it wisely. Use it in love and see the Universe open up to you. We are here to help and guide you.

> Only in love.
> And with much gratitude.

Week 6

Dreamtime

For a significant portion of your daily life
You rest your physical body
In a state of suspended animation.
These are the times that your spirit/soul
Is able to travel
In order to bring back knowledge
Or to help you process things
That have happened to you in your waking hours.
These are the times when you dream,
Though many of you are able to dream
In your waking states also.

Dreamtime is very important to your continued spiritual growth for the reasons just mentioned. But is there a way that you can better assimilate the knowledge, better process the feelings and experiences that are a part of your dreamtime? There is a way for you to begin down this path, so let us help you through this exercise.

You have heard many theories of how to interpret your dreams. For example, there is the study of the symbols that occur in your dreams. Certain objects are said to mean certain things. You may have been told to put yourself in the position of everyone who is present in your dreams, that each is a part of yourself. Both of these techniques are helpful and certainly worth exploring during your waking hours.

But where do you go and how do you receive this information that comes to you in your dreams? There are times that you travel far and wide, through the veil that is thinning at this time of the physical cycle. And so, you are able to pass into other dimensions, other planes of existence, and during those times you may have conversations with ascended masters who are willing and able to help you stay on your path back to the Oneness.

But there are many times when you only have glimpses of that which has transpired during this dreamtime. Or perhaps there are times when it is very difficult for you to wake or rouse yourself. These are the times that you can be certain that you have traveled, and though you may not remember clearly, the memory is stored in your subconscious.

It is for this reason that you can retrieve the information of the dream, to re-enact what transpired, if that is what you wish to do. It is your choice as to whether you wish to remember the entire dream or just the knowledge that was given to you through the dream.

In order to do this, sit quietly and breathe, in and out, in and out. Set your intent to consciously remember the knowledge that was presented to you during your dreamtime. It is not always necessary for you to remember the exact movements or activities in the dream. For sometimes these can be painful memories that you seem to relive during the dreamtime. The important piece is the knowledge or the beginning of the process that a dream might trigger.

Prior to lying down to rest, you might set the intent to consciously remember the knowledge received, or if you wish, the dream in which that knowledge was presented. It is all a matter of the intent that you set…pure, without fear or trepidation. For your Ego has much invested in keeping things exactly as they are in this moment, without any forward movement towards your conscious return to the Oneness.

After setting your intent, the key is just to allow the knowledge to come to you as you calmly breathe in and out, in and out. No forcing, no expectations. And remember, the knowledge is already there in your subconscious. It may just require some time to filter down into your consciousness. Until it does, trust your intuition, your *inner* knowing, for this taps into the knowledge that is present, just not yet available to your conscious mind.

Be gentle with yourself during these changing times. Dreamtime is very active for many of you right now. This is in preparation for the coming changes to your planet and to the entire Universal Being. If you experience ups and downs, know that this is happening to many, and that you are not alone in this process.

Allow yourself time to rest, to just be…without the constant bombardment of noise that surrounds you. How can you possibly hear your *inner* voice with all of the external din surrounding you?

> Trust yourself and your intuition.
> Understand that this process is occurring
> To many across this plane.
> And know no fear. Just love.
> Remember that is all that truly is.
> That is what you truly are.
> Love.

Week 7

What of...Memories?

You come within this human form as a spirit/soul
With a long life prior to embodiment.
You bring with you much knowledge
That has been collected across the Universe
By others like you who have chosen
To experience life in different forms.

The memories of that knowledge still remain within you. They are
just more difficult to connect to while in this physical state. For
that reason, it is important for you to allow yourself time to rest, as
this is the time that you can help bring back these memories, this
knowledge, to use in this physical plane.

If you only could understand the vast amount of knowledge that is
already available to you, there would be no feelings of inadequacy,
or need of acceptance or approval. For you would better understand
that you already are more than adequate – accepted and loved by all.

This physical realm is one of the most difficult planes in which to
exist because of the feelings of disconnect and separateness the
physical body creates. We cannot stress enough that this form which
you inhabit is similar to pieces of clothing that you apply to cover
and protect yourself.

Consider this. There are many on this plane who have had injuries
and had to learn once again how to speak or how to walk. The same
applies to each and every one of you. But for you, the lesson is how
to once again learn to fly, to soar. To use the depths of knowledge
already in your possession to lead you back within the fold, back to
the Oneness.

You often praise the explorers of this plane for seeking new adventures, going *where no one has gone before* in order to bring back the experience of those journeys. Can you understand that is what each and every one of you is doing right now in your lifetime here? You are doing exactly that.

And once again we say that you are doing it unselfishly, for the common growth of the entire Universal Being. Remember that when you are telling yourself, *'I am not succeeding, I am not worth loving, I am not contributing to anyone or anything.'* For you, in fact, are doing so much with every breath that you take. Remember that you are a part of something much greater than you could ever imagine in your current physical state.

Why do we stress this today? To encourage you to give yourself time to rest, to meditate, to just be. For these are the times when the connection becomes stronger. And as you do this more frequently, the knowledge will begin to come back to you. And in time, as you strengthen this conduit, the memories and the messages will begin to come to you, even in the din of your daily life.

But you must start as one who requires much practice and effort to relearn the language. The building blocks must be put back in place. And once they are, see how far you can climb with the memories that return to you.

Remember that you are all on the same path back to the Oneness. Each and every one of you has a different gift that will help you along the way. Seek to learn what those gifts are, and use them to move forward and to help others on their paths.

It is as if you all have a different piece of the puzzle to bring to the table. Individually, each piece does not reveal much to you. But when all those pieces are combined, a masterpiece lies before you.

Remember that your time here is meant to reconnect to the All. And along the way you might accrue much wealth, many experiences, and much power in this physical realm. But the true wealth, the true knowledge, the true power lies in your connection to the Oneness.

Remember, too, there is not one moment in your life when you are not loved, when you are not appreciated for who you are.

> You are *never* alone,
> And you are *always* surrounded by love.
> Always.

Week 8

Sadness and Loss

There is an air of sadness and loss
Across many nations
Here upon your physical plane.
And for those not immediately affected
By the events occurring,
Many are connecting to feelings of loss
Through the group consciousness.
It is at times like these
That the connection linking the All across this plane
Is so important.

In times of need, there are calls for support – physical, monetary and emotional support, all of which are important on this physical plane. What is also very important is the raising of the energies across this web of connection. We have told you of this before – how all are connected by this web. And so, the many feelings of anger, sadness, and loss will affect the group consciousness.

These are the times when the *give and take* of energies across this web becomes so very important. Now is the time for those not immediately affected to send out much positive energy. For the energy levels waver and fluctuate across the group consciousness. In order to continue the forward movement for all, it is important for strength, resolve and positive energies to flow into this web.

Remember that your thoughts, your words and your deeds affect what types of energies flow out and across the Universe. Do not allow the suffering of others to lower your energies at a time when you are needed to pulse positive energy into this web.

All are connected. *All* are connected. And for those of you who are more sensitive to the fluctuations of the group consciousness, we ask you to take time to rest and rejuvenate. This is a time for you, most importantly, to keep your joy and connection strong, so that you can help maintain the higher level of vibration across the group consciousness.

Now is the time for you to be in gratitude, in harmony and alignment with the Universal flow, in order to help those who are stumbling. Keep your energies high, so that you can contribute to the Universal flow. Your help is needed and will continue to be needed, as the forward movement continues across your physical plane.

Do not turn away at a time when you are most needed. Join us in holding others in light and in love during these times of Universal growth. We ask this of you and give our gratitude to you for your daily help.

Be the bearer of light that you truly are. Hold your light high and strong as others' may be flickering. Be at ready to rekindle the inner flame of others should they falter. Allow your brightness to shine forth. Help us to help you.

> And for those who may be faltering,
> Look towards the light.
> Allow the warmth of it to shine on your face.
> And find the joy that is present in your life.
> You are always surrounded by our love.
> Let us help you once again. Call on us.
> You are never alone.

Week 9

The Universal Song

Stop, breathe and listen to the music.
Can you hear it playing across the ethers?
It is not something heard with your physical ears
But with your heart.
The music is your roadmap to what is coming,
To where you have been and how to move forward.

It is a gentle, soothing music to which you can align your vibration, in order to be completely enveloped by it, embraced by it, soothed by it. But the din of your physical world is currently drowning out this gentle call to you. It is the call of the Universal symphony, which is always playing, for it is part of the larger web of connection.

Consider your whales and how they sing to one another in the waters of your oceans. This is exactly the way the Universe sings to you. But instead of an ocean of water, it is an ocean of energies, constantly in motion. For those who have heard it, they say it is the most beautiful sound, indescribable in human words. Do you not understand that this is *your* song? This is *your* language. One that crosses all barriers. All planes. All cultures. It is the Universal language, and it is your native tongue.

Close your eyes in silence. Clear your mind and gently begin to sway your body. That physical movement is in synchrony with the Universal melody. It is just your conscious mind that has not yet connected to it. Breathe deeply and allow the beat of your heart to match the beat of this gentle song. Be still and connect with the gentle rhythm of the Universal song and become One with the All.

The beauty of this music reflects the inner beauty of each and every one of you. For the Source of you and all beings is one of Light and Love. No matter what you experience here upon this plane, your Source is of Light and of Love. And it calls to you every moment of the day, as a mother bird calls to her fledglings. *I am here. You are a part of me. You are not forgotten. You are not alone. You are connected.*

Find the light. It is there in front of you. Follow the gentle tug of the Universal vibration. It surrounds you. It embraces you. It transforms you. Allow it to enter your life.

> You are not too busy.
> You are not unworthy.
> You are not unable to hear it.

For it is a part of your inner being. Your very soul rides on the waves of majesty. Understand who you are, who you *really* are. Your power is endless, your connection, secured, your love, complete. You are One with the Universal song. Listen, dance and be free. Let us sing to you with an outpouring of love and gratitude for your service to the All.

> For this, we thank you.

Week 10

Kindness

There is a gentleness that is present
Within each and every one of you.
It co-exists with strength and courage,
For both are often needed
In order for you to exhibit kindness or compassion.

There appears to be a perception here upon this plane that kindness
evolves from weakness, from lack of self-worth, from being an *easy*
target, when in fact, the exact opposite is true. For often, showing
kindness and compassion requires you to take a step away from
the crowd and to act alone. It often shows leadership and resolve, a
willingness to set the tone, to teach the lesson, to show the way.

Do not forget to show this during your daily life. It requires you to
step out of your comfort zone at times. It requires you to be aware
of your surroundings. It requires you to be present in the moment.
And is that not what we have taught you time and time again – to be
present in the moment?

For the present is all that is. It helps to create the future and heal
the past. What you do in this very moment is setting the stage for
the next one, while releasing hold on the previous one. Ah, if all
could only start each moment anew, think of how the world would
change! No regrets, no grudges, no expectations. Life as it is in all its
nakedness. Life in the now.

It is time for you to be kind to yourself, also. You have this season
of giving in celebration of a birth, a season for celebration and
reaching out. But should this season not be part of every day in your
life? We do not quite understand the focus on just one time of year.

Should not your every moment be one of celebration, giving and reaching out?

There is a great need at this time to spend time in silence and meditation, if only for a moment every day. It is during these times that you can connect with your Source, to renew and regenerate, to receive the loving kindness and embrace of the All. Do not forget to do this, especially at this time. This is our gift to you; your gift to yourself. Time spent sitting and breathing, walking and breathing, eating and breathing. Being aware. Being of One. Being of Love.

These short meditations can raise your spirit, raise your energy, and raise your connection. And that is sorely needed at this time. Allow the joy of you, the joy of the All to rise within each and every one of you. Celebrate your very existence, your every breath. Let us help you by allowing the connection to strengthen between us.

Be kind to yourself. It begins with you. You deserve it. You are worthy of it. And as you grow, the world grows brighter, the Universal song is louder, and the energies rise higher.

Sit in silence, walk in silence, eat in silence. Love yourself and exhibit kindness towards yourself and others.

For the gift is *you*.

Week 11

Reclaim Your Power

Gently. Firmly. Lovingly.
Reclaim your power that you have given away.
Reclaim your power that you have denied.
Reclaim your power in order to use it
In light and in love.
It is yours. It has always been yours.
It is a part of who you are.
Reclaim it and use it wisely and for the common good.

Each and every one of you is connected to the Source, and with that comes the power of creation – creating your world, your life, your perception of how things really are. Many of you feel unworthy and are unaware of how easy it is to change your life by how you perceive it.

You need not be victims to others, you are stronger than that. You need not live with fear in your hearts, for you are of love. The power you have is in how you perceive your world. Is it one of kindness and joy? Or is it one of fear? You have the strength to change your immediate life and draw either fear or love to you. And as more of you choose to own your power, ah, see how the world in which you live will change.

You are ready to acknowledge this power, to use it to perpetuate a loving world. It is time for you to cease your acceptance of a life filled with fear, with blame, with negative thoughts and actions. The change begins with you.

Remember that you are One with All, that you are connected to All. And with that connection comes the power of the Universe, not to be used for self-gain, for that does not truly exist but in your mind. But to be used to raise the energies of your world and of the Universe.

Change your perceptions of what you can do. Choose joy every day. Choose self-worth in every action. Choose positive loving thoughts over negative fearful thoughts. And see how your daily life changes. *You* create your world. *You* have the power to do so. Do not let others choose the world in which you live. Choose it yourself. Choose a world of love and kindness and see what that creates for you.

Remember that your thoughts are very powerful. They create your world. It is your choice to view your life as positive or negative. Choose love. Choose forgiveness. Choose to live in the moment. The past does not exist. The future has yet to be created. And it starts with the now.

Judge not yourself or others, for the lessons you have learned have brought you to this place where you stand in this very moment. Ask that your lessons be gentle as you continue on your path of growth and expansion. Do not minimize who you are and what you are capable of doing, of being, of creating.

Live fully in *this* moment, this perfect moment of existence. Breathe in love. Allow it to fill your lungs, your body, your entire being. You come from love. You shall return to love. Shed these dark cloaks of fear and dread. You have the power of creation in every moment of your days. *Every* moment.

Reclaim your power. Reclaim your joy. Be the source of light and love that you truly are. Be expansive in your joy, and radiate love to all who cross your path – no matter who they are. Feel yourself being uplifted as you do so. Can you feel the lightness returning?

Reconnect with your Source. The power is yours and has always been yours. And now is the time to reclaim it. For your light is needed to shine.

The light begins with you.

Week 12

Silence

There is much noise that surrounds you
And lives within you.
Think of your daily lives.
The hustle and bustle, the timers, the beepers,
The static, the machinery.
And then think of what fills your head
Every moment of the day.
Worry, decision-making, planning, analyzing.
Do you ever take the time to just listen?

The perception here is that individual success comes with monetary wealth, personal possessions, power over others, and status within your societies. But individual success does not really exist. How can it when you are a part of the All? When you are connected to all of existence, how can personal success truly exist? And yet you spend your days striving for a better place in society.

We understand that your society, particularly in the more developed areas, believes that monetary success makes your life easier. And we understand that many of those without that wealth suffer greatly. But is it not also true that many who have accumulated much wealth also suffer? Instead of pushing forward as your society has taught you, stop. And listen. All that you require in terms of knowledge, timing, and forward movement begins here...within the silence.

Come back to us by way of the silent path. Turn off your machines, worry not about tomorrow. Be present in the now. In silence. The din that surrounds you, which has permeated you, drowns out the silence and the knowledge that you seek. Can you allow yourself the time to be still? To be present. To be at-one.

You have become addicted to noise, to stimulation, to moving at such a fast clip, that you are missing the journey. Is the destination that you seek fulfilling when you reach it? How much did you miss in your efforts to get there? How many opportunities to experience joy and connection have you missed, as you have focused on the journey's end? Living isn't done in leaps and bounds but in small, quiet steps taken one by one. Allow yourself the pleasure, the joy, of the journey. In silence. As you listen to the inner voice, the connection, the Universal knowledge that awaits you there. Quietly.

By tapping into this well of silence, you will understand the dance of the Universe...that everything is moving exactly as it should...that Universal movement does not flow in measured increments of time. Instead, it is the coming together of multiple forces which allows you to take the next step. Do you not realize that each step you take is not taken alone, but in synchrony with much larger forces that surround you?

Listen. Can you hear the quiet beat of the Universal heart? Do not work against it with personal aspirations. Work *with* it in harmony with All That Is. How many do not know the next step that you should take? Tap into the silence. Allow yourself those joyful moments of just being. Surrounding yourself with noise and activity is not the way.

Instead, surround yourself in silence every day, if only for a moment. Allow it to caress and soothe your frayed nerves. Allow it to provide you with the answers you seek. Trust that it will bring you joy and connection, and leave the noise behind. Change your world.

It begins with you.
In a single moment.

Of silence.

Week 13

The Web of Connection

There is a clear web of connection
That touches all of existence across planes,
Which gives you the opportunity to be at One
In ways you have never imagined.

The time is now for you to better understand this connection, in order to nurture and better develop it. *The time is now* for you to better understand that you do not and have never stood alone in this world. *The time is now* for you to understand how your actions, thoughts and deeds affect the entire web of being.

You have a responsibility in your life towards others, towards the All, in your thoughts, your words and your actions.

The physical body creates an illusion of separateness between you and everything else in existence. This design was in order for you to find your way back to the Oneness, along with the collective lessons that you have learned along the way.

But many have lost their way and believe in complete separateness from the entire being of the Universe. The absolute truth is that you are and always have been connected to the Source of Creation from the first moment of your existence. You are *not* alone, and it is not even possible for that scenario to exist.

There is a Universal pulse that runs throughout all of existence. It flows through you, even as you are unaware of its rhythm flowing within you. There are moments when you have a flash of recognition of this Oneness of Being, but many discount it as a quirk of existence. When in reality, it is the *essence* of existence.

All are connected. Imagine the breath of existence flowing through each and every one of you and of all creation. Can you even begin to imagine this? Each breath you take is exhaled by another.

You are a part of something larger than this physical vessel, which you currently inhabit. You are part of a *whole*. The physical nature of your current existence was designed for you to pursue individual growth while also contributing to the whole.

It is time for you to better understand the connection between each and every one of you and with All of Creation. It is time for you to bless everything and everyone who crosses your path. For in essence, as you do this, you are also blessing yourself. It is time for you to help to raise the energetic vibration of this plane of existence.

When you feel sad or depleted, sit quietly and slowly raise your focus from within your physical body to a point just above your crown. Make this connection and allow the universal flow to fill you with loving energies. Understand that you are not a single cell of existence, but an integral part of a Universal whole. It is impossible for you to be alone because of this connection.

Take solace in this connection, for it is a loving connection, more expansive than you can imagine. And your existence matters greatly. Your contributions are necessary and valuable. Your very breath fills the entire Universal Being, every moment of your days.

Know that you are a part of something much larger than what many perceive in their daily existence here upon this physical plane.

Know that your contribution to the All is valuable and integral to the growth of the Universal Being. Know that you are incapable of being alone. How is that possible with the web of connection that flows between all of existence?

Ask for help if you are feeling depleted and alone. Call for help with no expectations of the response you might receive. Be open and receptive to the Universal love that surrounds and envelops you.

> Every moment.
> Every day.
> With every breath that you take.
> You are *never* alone.

Week 14

The Soul's Purpose

Before embodiment, your soul made a choice
To learn certain lessons during its existence
Upon this plane.
The choices were made
For the collective consciousness
Without emotion,
In a sea of love,
In a field of light,
In a spirit of unity and giving.

Once planted here upon this physical ground, the soul, while remembering its task, cannot always relay that information to the conscious mind. And so the human body, the conscious mind, the Ego, does not remember the contracts made, the motivation behind the choices.

Remember that free will exists, and you have a choice in what spirit you use your time here upon this plane. You may choose joy and compassion, or you may choose anger and judgment. The choice is yours, and the choice you make affects the All.

Your journey, your personal journey, is to find your way back to the Source with the cards given to you here, in this lifetime. The choices are yours in how you play that hand. No matter your choice, you continue to be a being of light and love. *No matter your choice.*

The physical body is vulnerable, with limitations. The soul is eternal. The loss of the physical body only allows the soul to move forward by another means. The connection is always there between you and others with whom you have crossed paths here upon this plane.

The connection is also present with those you have not physically encountered. Remember that you are connected to the All. *To the All.* It is impossible to break that connection.

The soul's journey from the human perspective is arduous and difficult. However, from a higher perspective, the soul's journey is joyous and free – done in love.

The actions of a single soul affect the All. The combined actions of many souls have an even greater effect on the All.

Choose to walk your soul's journey with a gentle step, and follow *not* the path of fear. Your time spent in your physical body is limited. Your time spent in light is never-ending. It is happening at this very moment, even though your conscious mind may be unaware.

Raise your vibration. Reach out and reach up. Choose light over darkness. Choose compassion over judgment. Understand that how you act today affects the All.

Take comfort from others and *give* comfort to others when needed. Your light already shines from within. Allow it to wrap itself around you and others. Allow your light to wrap around the entire physical world. You and your every thought, word and deed make a difference.

Accept the joy of who you really are, and share that with others. Shine the light from within to the world. Feel the love that surrounds you. Walk your soul's journey gently and with love. And if you stumble, we shall be behind you to catch you and set you back upon your feet.

> You are Light
> You are Love
> You are One.

Week 15

What of...Perception?

What is the true reality of this physical world?
How can you be sure of what is really happening?
If five people observe an occurrence,
You will receive five different versions
Of what happened.
Which one of those versions
Accurately describes what really happened?
All of them.

Each person views an occurrence from their perspective, which is filtered through their reality. What you may perceive as a gesture of gratitude, another person may perceive as a gesture of arrogance. Everyone has a different perception of life here upon this plane.

And so, what does that mean for you? How can you be sure of what has really happened? The answer is that you cannot be sure how anyone else has viewed the same situation. All perceptions are correct, because they are viewed from the world that each person has created. Your perception is colored by your reality, by your way of seeing the world – positive or negative. Conciliatory or vengeful. With compassion or with judgment. Your perception of any event will fulfill your beliefs of how your world exists.

Each and every one of you is a part of the All. Each and every one of you has certain lessons to learn for the collective consciousness. And each and every one of you has had different life experiences along the way to learn these lessons. Each lesson is valuable. Each experience is important. Each interaction that you have with others will help that person along their path back to the Source.

Observe life as you know it from a higher perspective. See the many possibilities, the many variances of how a situation may be viewed, and you will find that compassion flows easier within you. The Ego wants you to believe that life can only be viewed in one way... *your* way. There are as many ways to view the world as there are people in it. Understand that your emotional memories change your perception. Understand that there is only one true way to view an occurrence...with compassion and non-judgment.

The possibilities are infinite in how life in this physical world can be viewed. Be open and receptive to all possibilities, for all exist. Allow your higher self a voice in viewing your world. Understand that *you* create the world in which you live, and every one of you has created a different world. Join together in sharing your individual worlds with love, understanding and compassion.

> And see how gentle the breeze of reality can feel.
> Be of love. Be of light.
> Raise your sights.
> View your world from a higher perspective.
> And see how brightly it can shine.

Week 16

The Reflective Mirror

Stand in front of a mirror and what do you see?
A face too wrinkled, too tired, not attractive enough,
With features either too big or too small.
But when you reply with an answer such as this,
It means you are only looking
Through your human eyes
At a human vessel.

Look deeper. Look within the eyes that stare back at you. Now close your eyes and continue to look. This time look inward. What do you see? Is there a light appearing before you, a color, a matrix dancing on that viewing screen in front of you? How do you feel when you see these things? And you *will* see these, for they are there for everyone to see, including you.

If you do not see them at first, it is only because you are unaccustomed to *seeing* this way. You may say that you see only darkness, but look closer, for dispersed among that darkness are points of light, everywhere. Look closer and breathe. You are composed of light.

We have told you this many times before, but now it is time for you to begin to see the light within. See with your heart, not with your mind. Turn off the dialogue and just breathe. Settle into the breath, for just a few minutes. And as you do, pull the blanket of love closer around you. Envelop yourself with the warmth of the love that is everywhere. Pull it closer and allow it to heal your wounds, to soothe your frayed nerves, to swaddle you as a babe, to allow you to feel loved and protected.

And breathe. Inhale love for you, exhale love for all. Love in and love out. Love in and love out. Effortless, natural and healing.

For your natural state is one of light and love. The denseness of the human form creates the illusion of separateness and aloneness. You believe the illusion that the human form controls you and your life, when, in fact, it is the other way around. *You* control your human form, and you do it with how you allow your energies to vibrate.

As you breathe, surrounded by love, see all the atoms of your humanness begin to dance – to *dance* with *joy*...every atom of your being in motion, emitting loving vibration. And allow it to connect with the love enveloping you, as if two pieces of a puzzle have snapped into place, connected as One – your true and natural state.

Feel the connection. Feel the love. And so, the next time you see that human face reflecting back at you, see the dance, the flickers of light as they bounce off each other in their dance. And see the cloak of love that surrounds you. Every day, all day, without fail.

> You are Light.
> You are Love.
> You are One.

Week 17

Tears of Sadness or Joy

Shedding tears. You all do it.
It is an emotional release of sadness
Or perhaps even anger.
It is a mechanism of cleansing,
Of moving the emotions up and out
To once again bring you peace and inner calm.
For it is when you feel that inner calm
That you have the most clarity in your life.

The human vessel, though fragile, has many wonderful designs within it to help you along your way…and tears are one of those designs. The perception of this world is that shedding tears is a sign of weakness, when in fact, tears are strengthening and empowering.

Imagine those tears carrying the emotion from within – little drops of intense emotion moving out, making room for the love and inner calm that will soon replace that emotion. And often, after you cry, you sleep, allowing the body to transition from a state of intensity to one of acceptance, love and calming energy.

Remember, it is in those resting moments when you are best able to make and feel the connection with the loving kindness that surrounds you, envelops and heals you. It is during these moments of rest when your human mind steps aside, and your heart can once again spiral up to strengthen the connection with the All. The tears evaporate. The emotion is dispersed into the ethers. And once again you have cleared the space for loving energy to replace what has been dispersed. Call to it, invite it in and accept the love. Allow it to fill your earthly vessel to the brim with light, tingling with pure love.

Do not judge the ways of being. Instead, allow life to flow. Follow the current, and do not fight it by trying to swim upstream. Allow yourself to ride the waves, as they take you to your next moment in life. Trust not your head, but your inner compass. Close your eyes and navigate with that compass, without judgment, without preconceived notions. For indeed, you are able to fly higher, sing sweeter and love more deeply than you think. The mind limits you. The heart expands your horizons and is your rudder, as you follow the current of life.

Discard the map and trust the inner voice, for the journey has many paths, all leading to the same end. It is your choice which route you take. But know this. You will arrive at the same destination – back to the Source, the loving Oneness…who will be awaiting you with open arms, with tears of joy to have you back once again. Tears of joy.

You are Light.
You are Love.
You are One.
And *always* have been.

Week 18

Why Are You Not Listening?

Why are you not listening when we talk to you?
Why do you turn your head, lower your eyes, or walk away?
Why do you call to us, often in desperation,
Yet when we answer, you do not listen?
We are always with you. Always.
We hear your call to us
And we are there with a response.
Always.
But you do not seem to hear it.

And so we ask: *How do you expect to receive your answers?*

Do you expect an apparition to appear in front of you with the solution to your dilemma? Do you expect a rumble in the sky, a bolt of lightning to precede any words of wisdom and encouragement? Where and how do you expect to get your answers? Think about this.

The answers to your questions are always provided to you, but perhaps not in the way you expected them to arrive. The messenger might be a child with a simple question, a colleague's action that sparks a thought. Or, it might be a gut feeling, an urge to *go this way* or to talk with someone you just happened to see. The answers to your questions come in countless ways. They are not dramatic but are gentle and natural interactions.

Every aspect of your daily life has a message for you, but you must be open and receptive to the messages. Do not doubt your insights, your synchronous interactions with others. These are the ways in which we interact with you. This is how the connection flows throughout the Universe. Sudden, dramatic responses are not our way, for the message would be lost in the orchestration of the delivery.

This means that your awareness of all that happens during your day, being present in the moment, will allow you to *hear* your answers. And you may not realize that your answer arrived, until after you have awoken from a dream. After you have returned home and reviewed your day. After you have said good-bye to the person with whom you were speaking.

Do you not realize that *you are a part of us, and we are a part of you?* And so, your answers come from interactions with each other, as we are present with all of you.

The answers may come from any part of your life – animal, mineral, plant, spirit, thought… Change your way of listening. Be present and understand that *aha*! moment. Be grateful to the person who gave a part of themselves in order to be the messenger for you. Look everywhere. See everything. No action is too small to go un-noticed. Gentle messages. Quiet examples. Simple solutions.

Be quiet, be observant and be ever present in the moment. And understand also, that *you* are a messenger for others. You may not be aware of this role which you play daily, but it is one of your many functions here upon this plane of existence. As you all search for the path to follow back to the Source, you are an important part of the solution for others, as they are for you.

Synchronicity, co-existence and connection. Open your heart to the ways of the Universe. Take flight, soar high and sing sweetly. All are possible. For we exist within you and among you and always urge you to grow, to dance, to know the joy of life.

> Do not doubt yourself.
> Love.
> Practice non-judgment.
> And be present in the moment.

> This is your lesson for today.

Week 19

What of…Purpose?

A subject we have discussed before.
But well worth bringing up again.
What is the purpose of your being here?
Your life upon this plane,
With its difficulties, its joys, its limited time.
Why are you here?
And why is it so difficult at times for you?

You are here because you are needed here at this time, on this plane.
There are many changes occurring – changes that will tip the scales
as to the future of life here and in the entire Universe. Your presence
is needed at this time, in this place, to help make the necessary
changes. To help raise the energies and the vibrations. To increase
the joy. To contribute to the growth and healing of others.

You are needed here at this time.

How, you ask, *can I make a difference? I am just one person who struggles daily
with my own growth, my own issues and my own fears.* Yes, you do. But you
do not feel that way every moment of every day. And in those times
when you experience joy, lightness and freedom…those are the times
when you send out positive vibrations that surround you. Positive
vibrations that move out into the ethers to help raise the energies.
All of you are not at this level at the same time. For all of you are on
different levels on your path back to the Source.

But all of you *are* connected. And the more of you who are aware of
how the Universal connection works, the greater the effect on the
whole. Do you not think this scribe goes through times of struggle

and growth? And yet, it is the connection with all of you, the readers, which brings light into her life.

This happens with all of you. During a time of struggle, a glimmer of light shines on you from many possible sources – a playful pet, a loving child, a kind stranger, a beautiful sunset. There is beauty; there is joy present every moment of every day. And the more of you who notice this, the easier it will be for the masses to see this joy.

It is up to you, each and every one of you, to raise your own energies as much as possible, so that you can shine the light for someone else who is struggling at that moment. It is the power of the connection, and the more of you who can *see the light*, the easier it will be for those who live in fear.

You, in your life, are laying down the path for others to begin their journey back to the Source. *You*, in your life, are showing others the way. And *you*, in your life, are noticing more days of light than darkness because of others who shine the light for you.

This is your purpose here. The veil is thinning between worlds; the energies are rising. And much of this is because of you, no matter how insignificant you think you are.

> *You* make a difference.
> *You* are a part of the change.
> *You* are needed here at this time.
> Never doubt that.
> *We need you.*

And though you have no conscious memory of this, you agreed to be a part of this adventure at this time. To make a change. To be a part of the process.

So open your wings and soar, and during those times of struggle, do not judge yourself. For there will be a source of joy that comes to you to help you rise up again. Remember, this is still a human existence, and with that comes limitations. But do not forget that underneath it all, you are a being of Light and of Love who has chosen to be here at this time.

And for that, you have our eternal gratitude.

Week 20

Once Upon a Time

Once upon a time there was a tiny speck of light.
This speck of light was formed as a part of a whole.
This whole was a wondrous Source of energy,
Of light and love.
Which gave a part of Itself
So that the speck of light could come into being.

Born of the Source, yet able to stand alone. Always part of the
Source, yet able to return with lessons learned only in a life on its
own. An individual life with choices and decisions. Freedom to
explore. Freedom to grow. Freedom to experience things otherwise
unattainable.

As this tiny speck of light gathered these experiences, a watchful eye
kept a loving embrace around it. Grateful for the courage and ability
of this *piece of the whole* to go forth and gather life experiences, from
which others could learn.

That once upon a time is now. The story is your story. The life lived
is your life. A firefly dancing on a summer's eve. A star twinkling
in the heavens. A spark shooting off from a flame. One candle
among many, lighting up a darkened room. All of these images
could describe you, for first and foremost, you are Light. Created in
love. Connected to love. Co-creator of love. Every moment of your
existence.

You are not only connected to the Source. You are a *part of the Source*.
The light that shines within you, the light that is you, *is* the Source.
You are co-creator with the Source. You are co-creating as you
discover your path, your part in the growth of the All.

For the All is ever changing, ever growing because of you. Because of your experiences here upon this plane. Because you were willing and eager to seek out your own potential, to love and to grow.

Do you understand who you really are, from where you have come? Of what you are truly capable? There is not a Thee and a Me. There is only an Us.

And *We* are constantly growing, evolving and changing because of you.

> You are Light.
> You are Love.
> You are One.
> You are Ever-changing.

Week 21

Focus

Focus your attention on that which you cannot see.
Focus your attention on that which you cannot hear.
Focus your attention on that which you cannot touch.
Focus your attention on nothing.
For it is there where you will find your answers.
It is there where the wealth of knowledge lies.

How is this possible? In order to better grasp the purpose of your
being, you must remove the chatter from your life. It is important
to find a quiet space, where you can spend time in nothingness. The
activity of your mind, the chatter is *jamming the airwaves,* thus not
allowing the wisdom to descend.

It is in the nothingness where you will find the connection, long lost
to many, yet always there, quietly awaiting your return. For some,
the road has been circuitous. For others, the road has been a straight
path, intense at times. But for everyone the destination is the same.

You have a negative perception of nothingness, as if it describes
lack – lack of resources, lack of sensory perception or lack of
existence. When in fact, if you allow yourself to dive into the pool
of nothingness, you will experience the exact opposite of these
inaccurate perceptions. We are not talking about your physical
body, which is accustomed to the chatter, the sensory overload, the
constant yearning to be doing something, going somewhere.

This nothingness is part of a new journey which many of you are
now ready to begin. You may leave your physical body in a safe place
while your spirit/soul glides off into the void. This is a safe place to

be, but also a temporary place to visit, for you must return to your physical realm after touching down in the void.

As the veil lifts, more and more of you will experience being in both worlds at the same time. You might find yourself forgetting words, remembering dreams during the day, being more sensitive to your surroundings. This is all a part of your awakening.

But it is important to continue to stay grounded in this physical realm. Find a mentor, if you feel you need one. For when you are ready, your teacher or your students will come to you.

The nothingness has much to teach you, but do not get lost there. Visit for short periods of time, so as to become accustomed to its energies. Bring back the knowledge and use it here in this physical world. Begin to combine the worlds. You are already doing it, as you begin to better trust your intuition and not to second guess those moments of insight, of creativity, of sight.

The time is now for you to explore, if only for short periods of time. Ask for help, a guide to show you the way. Surround yourself with light before you journey and begin on the path to the void. Just five minutes in your physical world will feel endless in the void. Do not dally, for you still must tend your physical body, your physical world.

> And call on us to lead you, to guide you.
> We will gladly be there as you take your first step.

Week 22

The OM

The Universal sound.
The sound of peace and joy,
Of eternal light and being.
The sound of connection and knowledge.
The sound of the Oneness, the All.
The OM.

As you sit to begin your journey into the void, take a few deep breaths. Surround yourself in light and love, and produce the sound of the OM. This is your ticket to your passage into the void. Be not afraid. Set your internal clock for only five minutes, as you begin to test the waters of the eternal pool of nothingness. Be in a safe place, a quiet place, and be sure that your physical body is tended.

You *must* return to your physical body. You do not require a long time in the void to receive the knowledge that you seek. Call on us to accompany you and to guide you. We will not abandon you. But you must *not* stay long in the void. It is only a visit, a period of rest from the stresses of the physical world. A mini-vacation for your spirit/ soul to return to the nothingness from which you came. A brief homecoming. Joyous, peaceful and loving.

It is easy to want to leave your physical body permanently and rise into the nothingness. But remember that you have come into this physical world with a purpose, with a task to complete. In the process of acclimating to this physical world, many have lost that connection, that knowledge of being one with the All. Do not give up. Call upon us to guide you during your daily life. Allow time for us to be with you, to speak to you, to share our love with you.

It does not happen with all the chatter around you. Provide yourself some time to sit and be in connection with us, with the All. Provide yourself time to sit in the sound of the OM. Provide yourself the time to heal yourself, as you connect with your roots.

Surround yourself with love and light.
Set your internal clock for just five minutes.
Call on us to guide you.
Produce the sweet sound of the eternal OM.
And bathe yourself in the eternal waters
Of the nothingness.
Come back refreshed, renewed and re-connected.
It is time for you to begin your journey,
One small step at a time.

Week 23

Forward Movement

Your path is moving you forward.
Forward towards Divine connection,
Back to the Source.
The lessons which line this path
May sometimes seem insurmountable.
But always, you have help and guidance.
You have a connection with the Source.
Use this connection in your daily life,
Especially in those times of stress or despair
When you feel helpless.

Every step you take brings you closer to the knowledge that lies within you. Every step you take brings you closer to the light from which you came. Every step you take brings your vibration higher and lighter, more in sync with the Source.

Are you able to walk your path with the knowledge of loving beings with you, prepared to catch you if you stumble? Are you able to walk your path with the knowledge that you are never alone? Are you able to walk your path understanding that joy is present all around you, everywhere you look?

You say, '*I see suffering, turmoil and sadness. I see inner strife, war and greed. I see many things that do not appear to be of light and love.*' But all of these things are seen through human eyes. There is another way to see them.

Raise your vibration enough to see beyond these human situations. See the underlying light within each and every one of these situations. See the opportunities to share your light, to help uncover the light within all those around you. It is possible to change the flow of energies from negative to positive.

One person can make a difference across the spectrum of Universal light. One person. For each person is connected to the All. And so his/her actions reverberate along that web of connection. The way to begin is to hold your energetic vibration high. Practice daily to bring your vibration higher. Connect with your Source.

Once you begin doing this, notice the difference. The atmosphere in a room will change with your presence. Your higher vibration will raise the energy around you. It will be noticeable to others, though they may not be able to explain what they feel. You do not realize the power of this.

You need not have a solution for the problems of others. With your higher vibration, you allow them the opportunity to feel the difference. This in itself will help them to reach higher and to find their own answers from the Source.

Each and every one of you has the answers within. There is no need to go elsewhere, for the guidance is within. What you can do is to show others the way without judgment, without lectures. Show others the way by how you live your life, by how you maintain a higher vibration. They may not be aware of what they are feeling from you, but they will walk away feeling lighter.

Share the Universal energies with each other. Do not deplete your own energies while you become accustomed to this way of being. All you need to do is to walk in light and love. Surround yourself in light and love every day. Nothing else is needed at this time. Just this small gesture will begin to change the world around you.

> Others will notice.
> Others will follow your lead.
> Forward movement has begun,
> And it started with you.

> Many blessings to you for all that you do.

Week 24

Do Not Fear the Unknown

Why do you fear the unknown?
Why must you know everything that is to happen
Before it does?
Your future is evolving
And your actions in this very moment
Will change the outcome.
So then, how can you predict what will happen?
Is this not part of your learning process?

Your need to control, to *be prepared* for what is to come, is causing you much distress and elicits fear within you, if you do not know. You spend much time wondering and worrying about the future, when in fact, the future does not yet exist and depends on the present. In reality, there is no future, there is no past. There is only the *now*. And the now is where you should be focusing your attention.

We have talked about the web of connection and of the continuum. We have told you how everyone and everything is connected. With this knowledge in hand, understand the flow of creativity within and amongst you all. Understand how your energy, your thoughts, can and do affect what will happen next, not only in your life, but in the life of the All.

Thinking about the future and the past engages your mind. Being present in the *now* engages your heart. Have you ever lost yourself in an activity, focusing your complete attention on it to the extent that you forget the passage of time? These are the times when you are truly connected to the continuum as you stream with the collective consciousness in your present activity. During these moments, there is no emotion, no thought, just complete indulgence in your present action. While you are in this state, there is room for nothing else. There is no need for anything else. You are linked in to the continuum with full abandon.

In reality, there is no unknown in terms of meeting new people, journeying to a new destination, beginning a new task. For if you are a part of the All, there is knowledge in this connection available to you. Knowledge that you, as part of the All, have used before. But in order to tap into this knowledge you must get out of your head and back into your heart where the knowledge lies.

True knowledge, of Universal dimensions, lies within your heart. Knowledge of living in a physical world lies within your mind. This is the mind's purpose, to retain memories of how to exist on this physical plane. The trick is to combine these two forms of knowledge to move forward.

The veil is thinning, which means that more and more of you are living with a foot in both worlds. No longer will this *earthly* knowledge be enough for you to move forward. You have graduated to the next class and must now pull in the Universal knowledge to help you straddle both of these worlds simultaneously.

More and more, you will need to draw on the knowledge of the continuum to move through your day. Do not be afraid of this new way of living. You are ready. You have our support and help. Move softly and gently into the unknown. It is not dark and sinister, but filled with light and music and opportunity.

Approach your day with love and certainty that all is as it should be. Be present in each moment, moving forward with love. By doing so, how can the next moment and the next not be the same, filled with love? Love is all there is.

Release the fear from your mind. Open the window of your heart and allow the brightness of our world to fill your days. You no longer just exist in a physical world. You are now a part of both worlds, and for that we sing with joy. With open arms we welcome you and will guide you. Just ask.

It is just that simple.

Week 25

Self-Blame

How often have you blamed yourself for a series of events?
For the pain and suffering of others?
For an unwelcome outcome?
How often have you felt you were the cause
Of all that happened?

Remember that you are a part of the All. You are connected to the All, and any lessons learned are learned by the All. Remember that energy ebbs and flows as the waves of the ocean, between and amongst the All. This inter-connectedness is designed so that knowledge and learning encompass more than just one soul. Your lessons are inter-twined among each other. That is the way of the Universe.

For this reason, we ask you to understand the power of your thoughts, your words and your deeds. You are often the catalyst for change, regardless of your intentions. There is a tendency to self-judge if events, from your perspective, appear to cause much pain and suffering. Yet, in reality, there is no judgment, only forward movement from lessons learned along the path.

Remember that the purpose of your existence on this plane is the collection of knowledge for the All. Every moment of every day has a potential for knowledge to be gained. It is up to each and every individual how they attain that knowledge, how they react to the situation. Do you respond in fear or in love?

Rather than cast yourself as the perpetrator of pain and suffering, step back. Review the situation from a more detached level...from our level of view. Remove all emotion from the slate and observe how the situation unfolds.

You may have been a catalyst, but perhaps that was needed to begin the series of events that followed. You may have been the messenger or the benevolent instigator in an event that at first glance appears to be tragic or negative. However, this event is an opportunity for learning, for knowledge, and it is the choice of all affected as to how they will respond.

Will they point fingers and blame or will they step out of the emotion, roll up their sleeves and help each other over the rough terrain? Everyone has free will. There are many possible outcomes, and each possibility has different lessons attached to it.

Do not blame yourself. Take responsibility for your actions, indeed. But remember that the lesson, the opportunity for knowledge is an individual choice for all involved. Be pure in your intent. Know that each and every one of you has one of us whispering in your ear. All are loved. All are offered guidance. All are on a path towards the same destination.

Walk in light and in love. Honor your place in the world and in the unfolding of knowledge for the All. You are a part of a Universal web of connection. You are surrounded by light and by love as is everyone else around you. Allow the fear to dissolve, and step into the light. All will eventually arrive at the same destination.

Your actions provided an opportunity for change. You have done your part. Learn your lessons from the situation and allow others to do the same. Do not fear the outcome, for that has not yet come into being. The only moment is the *now*, and in this moment you are loved, you are Light and you are One.

> Allow joy to fill your being once again.
> Be present in your heart.
> Feel the love that surrounds you.
> It is always there in your heart.
> Breathe in and breathe out.
>
> Only love.

Week 26

Are You Ready for Change?

Are you ready for the changes coming to your life?
Are you willing to move forward without fear
But with love and anticipation?
Are you able to accept what is coming
As a gift for you and the world?

This physical world is not a static world. The Universe is not
static, but ever growing and ever changing. And as it breathes and
stretches its limbs, so will you grow and expand along with it. You
were not meant to find one little niche in life and remain there. Yes,
it is comfortable. Yes, it is safe. But soon the depth of knowledge
available to you must gently urge you forward. There is still so much
for you to learn. There is still so much for the Universe to learn.

Consider yourself to be as one of the famous explorers in your land,
going *where no one has gone before*. For the Universe to expand, this is
necessary for all to do. This does not mean that you will physically
move, though perhaps for some that is true. No, this means that you
will be gently led forward to try new things, to think in new ways, to
feel deep emotions that have not surfaced for many years. It is only as
you move forward through these experiences that the All can learn
from you, learn through you.

You are on a journey of self-discovery. You are at the lead of a
Universal adventure. But you are not alone in this journey. This is
a journey of self-discovery not only for you personally, but for the
entire existence of the All.

Touch your toe into the water for a moment and then dive in. Do
not be afraid. There is someone there at all times to keep your head

above water and to gently bring you back to shore, if you need a moment of rest. You have an energetic life preserver securely fastened around you at all times.

Can you do this with joy and a sense of adventure? As a child, were you not more willing to take chances, shrugging off the warnings of your parents to be careful? Be bold as you move forward, but also be aware. Stay grounded in your adventure and do not fly off into eternal bliss before your time. For there will be a time that you will return to the loving arms of the All, our dear adventurer of life.

Take a deep breath, wrap yourself in loving light and take that first step. You may rest in the comfort of your familiarity for a time. But then you will be gently reminded, gently pulled to move forward. Do you not wish to experience the sweetness of life in all of its possibilities? If you move forward with pure intent, with love in your heart, with fear banished from your existence, how could each step not be the sweet nectar of life?

Remember it is all in your perception of how events begin to unfold. As we see your life, all experiences are positive. That is not to say that if you are in physical danger that you should not remove yourself immediately. But remember that the lesson is always there, always present.

Can you live your life in joy? Is that not one of the biggest challenges you face daily, to see everything from a joyful perspective? We shall help you to change your vision from one of fear and dread, to one of joy and light. It is difficult, we understand, in this physical world of heaviness with the illusion of separateness.

Are you able to wake up each morning and say *'This is a day of joy, a day of connection, a day I walk with my guides supporting me every step of the way. This is a day of new experiences and new knowledge to be cherished and used for the highest good of the All.'*

Remember that your path ahead is filled with light to guide you.

Trust that inner voice which guides you. That inner voice is us calling to you, supporting you and loving you. In time, you will not even question what you hear, that intuition that urges you to do or not to do something. That is your internal compass, and soon you will allow it to guide you forward without a second thought. This is the Universal connection of which you are a part.

Walk your path gently and in love. Know that you are just one piece of the whole. You belong to something much greater than you can imagine.

> You are Light.
> You are Love.
> You are One.

Week 27

What of...Power?

Have you given away your power?
Do you allow others
To cause you to be happy or sad?
Have you forgotten who you are
And from where you have come?

One thing that has been difficult for you to learn here upon this plane is how powerful you are. You are connected to the All. You came into being when a part of the Source was given to you. Yet, every day, you allow others to determine if you are filled with joy or sadness. You take your cues from others rather than from within.

Perhaps you are afraid of the power that has been given to you. Perhaps you feel unworthy to be gifted with this immense amount of power. Perhaps you are uncertain how to use it in your daily lives. And so, let us begin by explaining this to you in terms that you will better understand.

Power here upon this plane is associated with wealth, possession, status and control. This is how you are taught of power and many of you see that power used for means of self-gain. Should you not be a person of means or status, you feel powerless in your daily lives.

The truth is that you have much power, but of a different nature. You have the power of love and connection, and this carries much more weight than the power you see in your world. Think of this.

You have the power to diffuse a tense and potentially dangerous situation by sending love and light, by raising your energies to envelop everyone involved. You have the power of connection to the All, where all knowledge lies in the collective consciousness. You have the power of inner peace and clarity in an outside physical world of chaos and din. You have the power to change this world, just by using all the gifts mentioned above.

The power you own is intangible and permanent. It is ever-present and is not something that can be taken from you. However, you often give it away freely and create for yourself a world of lack, of fear, of uncertainty.

Take back your power. This power is present in all of you. More power for you does not mean less power for someone else. That is only true for this power you have created in this physical world which feeds off of others. True power resides within.

You hold the power of how your day will be by how you choose to see it. You have the power to step back from emotion, blame, drama and to be of joy, knowledge and strength. You have the power of the connection of love. Which is more powerful, a connection made in love and service or a connection made in fear?

> You have all the power that you need.
> Use it wisely and daily and change the world.
> That is true power.

Week 28

How Do You Communicate?

What is your process for communicating with others?
Do you speak your truth
Or do you say what others want to hear?
Do you listen to their reply
Or are you only waiting for them to stop speaking
So you can speak again?
Do you know how to listen?

Everyone wants to be heard. They have something to say and want others to hear what it is. But what are they truly communicating? So much can be heard just in the tone of one's voice or in the stance of their physical body. So much can be learned from the look in their eye and where they focus their attention. What are they really saying?

You have learned here to allow your emotion to cloud your words and your communication. Once said, the words cannot be retrieved, as they go out into the ethers. True or false, the words have been spoken to be accepted or rejected by the recipient of those words. Often, the non-verbal forms of communication are much more telling of what a person is really thinking, of how they are really feeling.

In a tense situation, can you first take a deep breath before you speak? Can you surround yourself and those involved with light and love? Can you ask for help with the words that will come before you allow them to flow from your mouth?

Emotion, intense emotion, clouds your judgment, and often what you communicate is how you are feeling only in the moment. In times of intense emotion, can you just walk away until it passes?

Can you come back when you are grounded, connected and in a better position to communicate? You are not being asked to deny the emotion, for that must be felt and allowed to pass. You are being asked to wait until that emotion has passed before you discuss the situation.

There are many ways you have been taught to do this, to count to ten, for example. Another way is this. Breathe, feel your feet firmly on the ground. Imagine yourself as a tree and send roots down into the ground from the soles of your feet. Then take that intense emotion and send it down to Mother Earth. Allow her to take it and disperse it. You cannot ignore the emotion, but you can acknowledge it and then send it on.

After this, your vision will be clearer, your words truer. Your communication will be softer and better heard by the receiver. For you must remember that as you send out intense emotion, so does the other person feel that emotion and contribute their own, just adding to the chaotic energy. The result is that nothing is heard, for emotion clouds the interaction.

If you are a recipient of such emotion, do the same thing. Breathe and send that emotion received right down to Mother Earth. It does not belong to you, but to another. Be calm. Do not allow your emotion to increase the chaos. If you remain calm, watch how the situation evens out. By not matching the level of emotion coming towards you, there is no escalation. The other person will either calm down or walk away, for you have diffused the situation. You have the power to do this.

> Be present and know your truth.
> Understand the energetic component
> Of all interactions.
> Send love and light in your daily interactions.
> And see how your world changes.

Week 29

Listening, Hearing, Seeing

How do you listen?
What do you hear?
What is it that you see?
Is it reality or is it altered
By your individual perception?
Do you do this with complete abandon
Or do you give it only a part of your attention?

How much do you *really* pay attention to what is happening around you? Are your interactions distracted by cellphones, personal thoughts or judgments, by what is happening in another corner of the room? How much are you really missing because you do not give your full attention to these interactions?

Quieting the mind is not only a practice to be used in daily meditation. It is also a practice to be used throughout your day. How many of you say that it is difficult for you to be quiet and meditate because your mind wanders so very much? Think about how little focus you use in your normal interactions. Perhaps the first place to start in quieting your mind is in your everyday activities.

There are many distractions for you in your daily life with so much din and chaos in this physical plane. And as the veil continues to thin, as many of you begin to have a foot in both worlds, you will also have information coming from the other side. For this reason, it is important for you to begin practicing your focus in everything you do.

You have the term *multi-tasking* in which you proudly proclaim that you accomplished a large number of tasks within the same time frame. But how well did you complete those tasks? How much do you remember of what someone said, or of exactly what you did during that multi-tasking period? More and more of you are unable to remember what you did just a day before. Perhaps you blame it on old age, but have you considered that it may be lack of focus?

There is so much beauty here, to be seen, to be heard, to be felt, to be tasted. Not being present in the moment causes you to miss many opportunities for experiencing beauty. These are habits formed at an early age for many of you. And so, we would like to help you to better focus, not only in those quiet moments but throughout your day.

First, you must breathe. Stop, take a deep breath and feel it move throughout your entire body. Gather your personal energy that is scattered all around you and pull it back within you. Imagine this in any way that best suits you, using a vacuum cleaner –like movement, or imagining a large pair of hands gently collecting your energy and bringing it in closer.

The goal is to bring your energies in closer to your physical body so that you do not feel so scattered. Even though many of you are not aware of this energy field on a conscious level, you are aware of it on a subconscious level. Think of your phrase, *gathering my thoughts.* This is exactly the same process. Are thoughts not made of energy?

Once you gather your energies, pull them into your body and send them down to your feet, through your soles and into Mother Earth. We have mentioned this before, to feel as a tree with your roots extending down into the ground. Once you have done this, check and see how you feel. There will be more calm, more focus, and more strength. Practice this before you enter a room, before you begin a conversation, before you start an activity, and see how your life changes.

Replace your gadgets with a deep breath of connection and centering. Allow yourself the full experience of life here in this physical world.

Listen, hear, see, taste, feel.
And love.

Always love.

Week 30

What of...Action?

Are you stuck, unable to move forward?
Do you feel the weight of the world upon your shoulders?
Do you say *'I just cannot do this anymore?'*
Are you tired of trying?

Dear One, read these words. They are for you. They are to help you continue to move forward on your path towards the Oneness, towards the Source. Do not feel there is no forward movement, for there is. Every day of your being.

More and more of you feel mired down in the weight of the world and do not notice the little things that happen as you move through your day. The tendency is to focus on the heaviness, on actions which were not completed. But what of that which did occur? Was the focus on how *much* was done or on *how* it was done?

Review your day. Can you honestly say that your actions were done with pure intent? Are you able to look back on what transpired and remember a moment of peace, a small action of gentleness, a moment of loving interaction? These are the moments to be remembered.

Your daily tasks seem endless and are considered important in this physical world. But what is important in the Universal world is not *what* you did, but *how* you did it. Not how many of those endless tasks you completed, but your frame of mind while doing those tasks. These are the important aspects of life – not the quantity, but the quality, the intent and loving effort which was used.

Do not rush through an action in anticipation of another, with worry of how it will all transpire. Know that if you have focused your loving intent on the present task then you have completed it in the most perfect way. Know that all that matters is the moment, the current moment. Do not allow your worries about what comes next to come into your mind, for all that exists is the moment of now.

Relax, breathe, and feel the ground beneath your feet. Feel the connection you have with Mother Earth. Understand that you are being supported by her, every moment of your day. Her strength flows through you, up through the soles of your feet. Her solid strength is there for you to gather throughout your day.

Breathe in the air around you, and pull in the loving embrace of the Universal beings surrounding you. They are with you always. You are never alone. That is impossible, as you are connected with the All.

Remain in gratitude for each breath, for each step you are able to take. Live in gratitude daily. Your daily tasks may not be something you can change today, but the way you approach them is entirely your choice. Approach your life in loving embrace. Acknowledge the loving support beneath you and around you.

This is the first step on which you should focus. And after you have succeeded in changing how you approach your day, then you shall be ready to carefully choose and prioritize your day. Once you learn to walk and breathe in love, see how the importance of many tasks diminishes.

Do not cloud the beauty of your current life with worry about what has not been completed. Move in love from one moment to the next. That is enough. For love is all that is. Love is who you are. Love is the make-up of the entire Universal being.

> Be of One.
> Be of Love.
> Be of Joy and see the beauty of your life.
> See your own beauty reflecting back at you.

> And smile.

Week 31

Forgiveness, Understanding and Growth

Are you able to forgive
What seems the most heinous of actions?
Even without completely understanding
The motivation behind those actions?
Can you disperse that deep emotion felt
And come back to center?

You are not responsible for the actions of others. You are only responsible for your own actions, words and thoughts. Although there is certainly a connection and exchange of energy between you and all of existence, the immediate concern you must have is with your own actions. For change begins with you and the energy you send out into the world. It has a much greater impact than you realize.

There are occurrences upon this plane with which you do not agree, which may cause you much pain and emotional turmoil. For this, we understand, as many of these actions do not follow the lessons which we teach. However, please remember that All are connected. Judgment, condemnation and prolonged anger do nothing to move the collective consciousness forward.

Emotional reactions are a human condition and help move you towards action, either positive or negative. They are the catalyst for growth, for change, in either a forward or a backward direction. When you feel these emotions, we ask that you not hold them close for long periods of time. Instead, allow these emotions to be the catalyst for positive change in the world.

Only through love and forgiveness, kindness and compassion, joy and awareness of the inter-connection of All will you be able to grow closer to the Source. You may not understand the reasons for the actions of others, but that does not mean you cannot respond after a time with a positive action.

Do you not see how the negative actions of one often bring out the best in another? It is the give and take of love that moves you forward. This loving kindness is present in each and every one of you. Focus on that, rather than on the negative catalyst that caused the outpouring of love.

There will come a time when loving kindness will be ever present in your world. It will be a time when these expressions of love will be a daily occurrence, and not only in response to a negative deed. Start now. Begin today in changing anger and judgment into forgiveness and love. You need not understand the reasons of others, for often they are beyond your comprehension.

Allow your negative response to pass quickly. Move into a higher vibration of love and action. This is how you become part of the forward movement of your world. This is how you show others the way of being. This is how you contribute to the loving kindness ever present in your world.

> Do not walk in fear and anger.
> Do not look for suitable punishment and retribution.
> Walk instead in light and love.
> Show others the way of being.
> Be the example of forgiveness and compassion.
> Change your world…with gentleness, forgiveness
> And love.
> Allow your light to shine in times of darkness.
> And call on us when you need help.
> You are never alone.

Week 32

What Do You Want?

Do you know what you really want?
What would you do if you received it?
Would you sing with joy and embrace the gift?
Or would you shudder and say you are not worthy
Or not yet ready to receive it?
What do you really want?

Are you clear in your intentions when you think about what you want? Or do you waver back and forth, unsure of the details of your desires? Are you certain that you do not have misplaced longings?

Sometimes your desires are couched in terms or images that are not correct. You say you long for a certain thing, but if you really think about it, you are unsure if that will satisfy your cravings. Think of how often your physical body is hungry, and yet nothing you eat seems to satisfy. Is it not well known that when some are depressed or lonely, they eat to fill the void? But the cravings are not satisfied in this physical manner, for the cravings are for the feelings of love, connection and attachment, and not really for food. Those are misplaced longings.

Can you be honest with yourself about what it is that you truly want? Follow through on the image in your mind, and see what you do when you receive what you desire. Are you able to move forward using that new-found gift for the betterment of your life and perhaps the lives of others? Or are you unable to continue with the dream because fear and uncertainty have moved into the picture?

As you begin to move forward, you will notice that what you desire is more easily attainable, however strange that may seem to you. You will notice that the thoughts that continue to reside in your mind are suddenly manifested in the physical world. Because as you begin to walk the path back to the Source, your thoughts and your words become more powerful and are more likely to become a reality. Your calls go out into the ethers to bring back what you say it is that you desire.

Do not hesitate to believe this, for it will happen. But be prepared to receive that for which you ask. That is how it works in the world. If you do not receive it as you expected, then think of how you projected your desire out into the ethers. Be clear in your intent and your desire in order to receive exactly what you want.

Be responsible, as you begin to walk this path, in what you desire and how you ask for it. It is only a matter of time before it arrives on your doorstep, invitation in hand, waiting to be welcomed into your life.

Understand the power that is yours. Accept that power. Be not afraid of it, and use it wisely and for the highest good of all. Remember that your innate power does not take away from another's power. You each have your own individual gifts, and when you join each other to combine those gifts, you can change the world. Imagine the power in that.

Imagine.
Create.
And begin to change the world.
You will always have our help and support.

Always.

Week 33

Fear

Are your actions driven by fear?
Do you take the safer path
Out of fear of the unknown?
Are you holding yourself back
Because you are afraid of failure?

You hold unlimited power in your hands, in your heart, and yet, you continue to allow fear to drive your decisions. If you have accepted any of the tenets of these writings, then you should begin to understand that there is nothing to fear. Have you considered what the motivating reason is for your choices made out of fear?

Does not Ego come into play when you say you have a fear of failure? Do you not understand that every move you make is a move forward, and there is no possible way that you can fail? Of course, your vision of the end result may not be reached. But perhaps your vision was too limited, and your actions have a broader result. Until you allow yourself to be free of fear, you will not be able to step back and see the larger picture.

Do you avoid an encounter, a conversation for fear of hurting someone's feelings or perhaps of being wounded yourself? Indeed, if there is physical danger, do not pursue. However, in any other encounter, if you act with pure intent, are you not engaging in a worthwhile interaction? You cannot predict another's reaction or response to you. You can only walk in truth and love. And remember that in your daily life, this physical plane is meant for learning and teaching by or for you.

Use your intuition daily in your interactions. Understand how the timing of the Universe works. Do not respond or act out of raw emotion. But allow yourself a moment to breathe and center yourself before you enter into a pivotal interaction. Worry not about the outcome and move forward in love.

Fear will hold you back, anchoring you with heaviness when you have the ability to fly, to soar to new heights and dimensions. Unzip that heavy cloak of fear which burdens you and prevents you from moving forward. Allow it to drop at your feet, step over it. Shake out your wings and fly.

Can you feel those wing buds on your back, just beginning to form? Check them every day and feel them become larger and more beautiful, until they are an expansive pair of wings with which you can soar above the fear beneath you. You are so much more than you could ever imagine.

Begin today. Begin at this very moment. Breathe. Release the shackles of fear. Walk in love. Do not limit yourself or your vision. Think broader, fly higher, reach further than you ever imagined. This is only the first step in your awakening. Do not let fear hold you back. You will be astonished at the possibilities. And we shall applaud your initial flight to freedom.

> Do it now. Take the chance.
> You are never alone. We are always there to help.
> Just call upon us, your cheerleaders, your supporters,
> Your partners in changing the world.
>
> It begins with you.

Week 34

Your Daily Practice

Now is the time for you to begin your daily practice
Of forgiveness, gratitude and silence.
It need not be for more than a moment
During the course of your day.
But in doing this as part of your day
You will find a shift occurs for you.
A shift towards peace and freedom.
A shift towards clarity.
A shift towards strength and knowledge.

Have you noticed how a day of intense emotion leaves you completely exhausted? Have you noticed how the mental replay of misdeeds done to you or by you removes you from the present? How this keeps you from experiencing the beauty and joy that is present in the now? Have you yet begun to understand how taking that moment to breathe and center yourself fills you with inner strength, making you feel more secure in where you stand right at that moment?

By being aware of your immediate surroundings in present time, you are connecting with the All. The first step in this practice is to begin to dissolve Ego, which holds you in your mind and closes you off from the present. Ego always remembers the past, plans the future and makes comparisons between thee and me.

Allowing oneself to be present in the now removes power from Ego. It allows you to start fresh, as a young sprout, tender and green, opening to the light, vulnerable but with an inner strength that lies deep within its roots. You are that sprout, and it is time for you to move towards the light, knowing your inner strength is there to help you stand tall, no matter what. As with that sprout, you have the anchor of strength within and the light above welcoming you to grow. Take a chance. Breathe, trust and allow your inner beauty to unfold.

Begin by pushing through the hard seed casing you have used for protection. With purpose and resolve, move through the darkness as you begin to sprout, moving upward towards the light. It is when you allow the light to shine upon you that you begin to move towards your full potential. Can you find the resolve to allow yourself to be vulnerable in order to grow? Even in that dark loam, there are nutrients to feed you, water to sustain you and warmth to embrace you as you find your way.

So too in your life. But you must make the choice to grow towards the light. Use the simple daily practices we offer to you. Approach each day with no memory of the past. Harbor no judgments against others. For if you are growing and changing every day, would that not be the same for others? If you treat others anew each day, will not the old ways of being with each other begin to change?

In your relationships with others you have established a dance to which all parties have learned the steps. But what happens if you change the cadence? Everyone then, must adjust to the new rhythm to continue the dance. But the dance is not the same, because of you. Do you understand that change begins with you? For others cannot respond to you in the same way, if you have changed how you approach your day.

Start today. Right now. Begin a daily practice of forgiveness towards all, including yourself. Of gratitude for all aspects of your life and the lessons contained within each interaction. Allow yourself just a moment of stillness to gather yourself and feel your strength and connection. Then you can move onward and upward. You have more strength than you know, more power than you realize. Use both to change your life and to change the world.

It is possible.
It is simple.
Just breathe
And live
And love.

Week 35

Only You

Only you can change your world.
Only you can accept the love offered to you.
Only you can create a life of joy and bounty.
It is up to you.

Understand that the power to change your world lies with you and no one else. For no matter what another does for you, the final decision to accept the gift, the joy, the love, is yours. It begins with self-love and acceptance of the power and strength that is yours. You can give it away, which many of you do every day. Or you can use your power to make a shift in your life starting at this very moment.

How do you give away your power? Perhaps we need to give you a few examples. Do you worry what others think of you? Do you allow the actions of others to cause you great emotional distress? Do you require the approval of another before you make a decision? Do you think others are better or smarter or more worthy of love and success? Do you associate with others who constantly criticize you?

Often the life you lead is so habitual, that you do not even realize how you give your power away every day. So, stop. Review your life and ask yourself if any of these examples resonate with you. And if they do, begin to make a change without judgment, without drama, only with joy. Give gratitude for the lesson and gently move on. For remember that all are growing, all are changing, and all deserve loving kindness whether given in person or from afar. Each and every one of you has your own individual power and for that reason, you do not require another's power to move forward in this world.

All the knowledge you need is within you in the connection that you have with the All. That does not mean you should not discuss with others, interact with others or seek advice from others. But the final decision, the final choice should be your own, regardless of what another thinks. You cannot make a wrong choice because every choice provides a lesson learned. Do not agonize over a decision. Breathe, go within and sit with the possibilities. Then move forward with pure intent and trust that all will unfold as it should.

The connections that you have with others affect the result of your choice, and you cannot predict the outcome. You can only move forward with pure intent and joy. Be open to the lesson that results and know that each step you take brings you closer to the Source.

Remember that you are here to learn and grow. Each life is important in what it contributes to the collective consciousness. Trust your intuition, for that will guide you on your path. Do not harshly judge yourself or others for actions taken, for decisions made. For every step you take affects another on the web of connection. And somewhere along that filament of connection, your action made a difference. Your decision taught a lesson.

Trust yourself. Move forward with pure intent. Walk gently but firmly forward, and see how you can change your world.

> Only you can do this.
> Today, in this moment, choose joy.
> Choose to reclaim your power, gently and with love.
> Know the joy of self-discovery.

> The possibilities are endless.

Week 36

What If?

What if you ceased all worry?
What if you began to smile more often?
What if you took a deep breath every few minutes?
What would happen?

Do you realize how much time, effort and energy goes into worry? Worry about things you cannot change. Worry about possibilities that are only that, possibilities. Worry about the past, the future. Have you ever considered the fact that you rarely worry about the immediate present? This is the time of action, the time of now, the time currently unfolding in your life.

The only time that exists is the present. The past is over and done, the future yet to unfold. So then why do you spend so much time and energy focusing on something that does not even exist? Imagination is a tool that feeds creativity. However, imagining something in your mind and just allowing it to sit there and gain strength is not productive. The present is a time of action and the only time over which you have control of your actions, control of *your* actions, not those of another.

Memories are teaching moments. How they make you feel tells you whether you acted from your heart or out of fear or anger. They are tools to show you how far you have come or what you should consider changing.

Can you understand the continuum of your life?

- Actions taken.
- Memories of those actions.
- Reflection on change of actions or not.

- Actions once again with hopes of different or similar outcomes.

The key word in this continuum is action, which can only occur in the present, for that is all that exists. You have no control of the past or the future, only of the now. Acting with pure intent is all that needs to be done, and if intent was not pure in a past instant, then it can be pure in this very instant.

There is a reason why memories are forgotten or are different for everyone involved. The lesson has been learned and so the memory no longer fills a need. Individual memories of the same interaction differ because each participant has a different lesson to learn from that interaction. And once the lesson is complete, the emotional charge will dissipate from that memory. And soon, the memory will cease to exist, for it is no longer necessary for growth.

The present is all that is real. The future has not yet occurred. And how your life changes from moment to moment is dependent on the web of connection and on how you choose to manifest the future. In the school of life, the past is the textbook, the present is the test, and the future is the result of how much you have learned from that textbook. It is the continuum of life dependent only on what you do *now*.

So smile and see the beauty around you. Take a deep breath and center yourself. Worry changes nothing, only action moves you forward and your destination changes with each passing moment.

You cannot be sure of what will happen. You can only be sure of how you will be in the moment. And as you become more accustomed to acting with pure intent, the future matters not.

> For you can be certain
> That pure intent in action
> Is all that is required
> To move forward
> In light and in love.

Week 37

Common Threads

Are you really alone in this life?
Is it possible to separate yourself from others?
How do you choose to live this lifetime?

There is a common thread that runs between you and all of existence. It is not something you can shake off or disconnect. It is the way of being. You can ignore this connection that you have or you can acknowledge it, bless it and draw from it to help you through your day. The choice is yours.

The knowledge of the entire Universe is available to you. That is not to say that you can accept it in its entirety at one time. The human body is not capable of receiving that amount of information. This knowledge is revealed to you as you move forward on your path. You will not receive the knowledge if you are not ready to receive it. This is a part of your growth.

And although you are all connected, you are all individuals on an individual path with your own lessons to learn. But understand that as you learn your lessons, you are teaching others. You may do the bulk of the work in learning from your experience, but parts of that knowledge filter on down to others with whom you connect. You cannot underestimate the influence you have on others with whom you interact every day.

You, in your Ego, think that no one is watching or listening or caring about what you do or say. When in fact, every action, every thought, every word is affecting someone else along the spectrum of connection. You may live alone, you may work alone, but you are never alone and never disconnected from this common thread. Find comfort in that fact. Take responsibility for that fact.

You are a piece of the whole, and it is not possible to disconnect. Just as one who has chosen to amputate an injured limb continues to feel that missing appendage, so too, are you always connected in life with others. You may not be in their physical presence, but that connection remains strong and true.

Consider your vibration to be one string on a universal harp. This combined with the vibrations of all others creates the universal song. The waves of this universal song play throughout the entire existence of being. If one string becomes discordant, the others will compensate to continue the song that plays continually throughout existence. There will be a time that you will be able to hear this song, if you have not already done so.

Understand the connection you have and the song that you create every moment of your day. Allow the connection to lift you up when you feel unable to do it yourself. Sit in a quiet space, and allow your physical body to sway to the rhythm of your song. It is playing every moment of your day. For you. For all of creation. Allow it to carry you on its waves back to the Source.

> You have a part in this.
> Play it well.

Week 38

Moving Forward

Do you measure your success
By how far you have travelled
Or in the path which you have taken?
Do you breeze past opportunities
To connect with others
In order to reach your destination?

How do you move through your day? Do you dance with a light
step, or does the effort to lift your foot require all of your energy
and focus? You can change this dynamic very easily with a very
simple act.

Stop. Breathe. Feel the ground beneath your feet. See the light above
you and invite it to surround you with its loving embrace. Allow it
to fill you with warmth, and feel the surge of energy in your veins.
Allow yourself to feel the caress of love that is there for you. Allow
it to light up every cell within your being, and accept the joy that it
brings.

See your day ahead as a day of lightness and joy. Feel that, really feel
that possibility in your heart. Give gratitude for inner peace and
clarity. Smile. Hum your favorite tune and listen for the universal
song. It will not come through your electronic devices, but through
your heart. Can you feel the vibration of it soothing your frayed
nerves? For all is as it should be, and you are exactly where you need
to be in this moment. Allow the connection to move you forward
effortlessly as you glide to your next destination.

The weight of the world is not upon your shoulders. There is no
need to wear that heavy cloak of responsibility and control. The only

responsibility you have is to come from love. The only control you have is whether or not you act with pure intent.

Realize that you are but one drop in the ocean of life. You are part of the whole. And the waves of movement are not controlled by you, but by the combined movement of all that surrounds you. Think of how you can change the lay of the land by being an instrument of love – by providing the building blocks of a solid foundation for others.

Think of the power of the ocean and the contrast between a gentle tide slowly transforming the shore and a forceful wave causing drastic change in one powerful surge. Both affect the landscape, but of which scenario do you want to be a part?

The world will change as the Universe expands in its collective consciousness. There is only forward movement. The path that is taken is your choice. You have free will to decide how you will allow your life to ebb and flow.

But you are not alone in this current of life. Allow the love which surrounds you to lift you gently and carry you forward. Allow this gentle current to take you further than you ever imagined. The possibilities are endless. The love is constant and always present. You are one very important part of an infinite whole which ebbs and flows as the ocean tide.

> Be of Light.
> Be of Love.
> Be One with All of Thee.

Week 39

Healing

Have you considered the possibility
That healing happens every day?
Heal thyself.
Accept the gift of it.
Release your thoughts of old
And allow the light to shine in through your wounds
To mend, to heal and to make you whole again.

The possibilities in your world are endless. The limitations come from you and your way of thinking. Change is possible every moment of the day. *Every* moment. And understand that if you can create that shift, so is it possible for others in your life to do the same. It is a matter of choice. Allow the possibility of healing in order to grow in your immediate world. If more of you accept this, can you see how the world could change?

You carry physical, mental, emotional and spiritual wounds as you walk through your day. The burden of these wounds weighs you down, so that your steps are heavy and slow. Can you allow in the light to shine on those wounds to begin the process of healing? Can you change your way of moving through your day from one of battle to one of acceptance and love? Those scars can heal, but it must begin with how you see your world. Is it a battlefield or a playground?

We have said before that your life here on this plane is one of learning for yourself and for the collective consciousness. And we understand that often those lessons can be difficult for you. To ease the pain of those lessons, accept the outcomes, release the hardened memories and allow the light to shine.

Today is another day. A day filled with endless possibilities of joy and laughter and love. Stay in the moment, that fresh new moment beginning to unfurl. A moment in which you have the choice to see light or to see darkness. If it is difficult for you to see light and joy, try to do so only for one moment. Ask for help in allowing the light to come through. Imagine that old wound being healed with the light from above. There may not be a cure, but healing is guaranteed.

Imagine lightness of being. Imagine the joy of discovery. Understand the strength and the power each and every one of you has. And you have that now – you have always had it. You may just be realizing your strength now, as you consciously begin walking the path back towards the Source.

Understand the potential in every moment. What happened just a second ago no longer exists. Do not hold on to it. For there is a new moment, now, in which you can change your way of thinking, your way of seeing, your way of loving. There is always another chance for you. Endless chances throughout your day. That is the gift of this life for you. Can you give this gift to everyone in your life? The gift of new possibilities of interaction and of love.

Use your strength, your intuition, your connection to the All to move forward. The outcomes may not be what you expected. But whatever they are, it is *how* you accept them, *how* you learn from them, whether you hold them close or release them, that will create your day. And it will be a day of either light or darkness. The choice is yours.

>Choose light.
>Choose freedom.
>Choose acceptance and release.

>And allow the light to shine.

Week 40

Care for Thee

You are responsible for thyself.
Allow the love to flow through you,
Inward then outward.
That source of love awaits your acceptance.
Hold it close, wrapped around you
And feel the healing begin.

Never think that you are alone, stranded on a wasteland with no resources. The truth is that you have love surrounding you and within you. It is bountiful. It is never-ending and it is your make-up. You can tap into that love at any time, any place, with only a change of your perspective.

But first, you must acknowledge that you are worthy of this love. This is something many of you do not do. How can we impress this upon you? There is a disconnect between you and your higher self. First you must re-establish this connection.

To do this, sit comfortably, close your eyes and breathe. In and out. In and out. Slowly. Gently. Without thought. Without judgment. Feel that breath of air move throughout your body. Now imagine that breath washing away the internal darkness that has begun to take hold within you. Each breath clears out a tiny portion of your heart, your mind, your fingertips. Every breath permanently removes a small piece of that inner barrier constructed over the years. And as those portions are removed, a bit of light is able to come through, just as through a window freshly cleaned. That light is healing light filled with love for you and the All. It moves both ways, both inward and outward. There is a pulse of love with every breath moving through you and outward.

The time is now to accept your brilliance. Do not doubt that you shine with the brilliance of a star in the heavens. For that is how we see you, that is how we find you, through your light. And we see each and every one of you. None are missed. None are forgotten. For we can see the light that you have yet to find within yourself. Trust our vision of you. See with our eyes. Love with our hearts. Speak with our gentle words. Walk with our love surrounding you, enveloping you, carrying you forward to your next destination.

Allow your wings to unfold, as a fledgling in preparation for flight. Understand that you can soar above the mundane, the self-doubt and the fear. *You* are a vessel of love, Universal love. And you are strong enough, big enough, worthy enough to contain it and share it with the world.

> Begin with loving yourself.
> Allow us in to help you.
> The time is now
> To begin to see the beauty that you are unfolding.
> The time is now for you to shine.
> Do not doubt our vision of you.
>
> Thy love begins with thee.

Week 41

The Healing Has Begun

Laugh, sing and dance with joy
For the healing has begun.
Slowly, but steadily you have begun
To walk the path back to the Source
And, oh, how the heavens sing,
Ready to embrace you once again.

Unbeknownst to many of you, there is a squad of cheerleaders urging you on. Each and every one of you has your personal group of guides, who are lovingly waiting behind the scenes, as you step out onto that stage of life. They are there to whisper to you the lines you may have forgotten. They are there to direct you to stage left or stage right. And they are there to applaud you for a performance well done. They do not judge you as you judge yourself, for they only see your brilliance. They know from where you have come and to where you are going. They are here to guide you back. They are your own personal GPS with a preset destination. Home.

Can you feel the lightness in your step, the bounce in your walk, the song in your throat? All are present, ready to be uncovered by you. The world awaits your transformation. The world needs your transformation. And you are ready, for the healing has begun for you, and for the world.

Feel the excitement in the air. Feel the anticipation of the wonderful changes already beginning in this world, your earthly plane. It begins with you, and you have taken the first step.

This is our mission, one which we accept with love and excitement. How can we not be thrilled to see the internal light of every one of you begin to shine brighter, as you accept who you really are? Just as a parent watching a child on a journey of self-discovery, we are watching you with joy in our hearts for the changes that have occurred, and for the changes we know are coming soon, very soon.

Connect. With each other and with Mother Nature. Connect in your daily lives. Acknowledge the sacredness of every form of being, and understand that you are a part of the All. As the energies begin to rise upon this plane, you will better understand this connection, this sacredness of being. And enough of you have begun the journey, that the changes have begun. We have awaited this moment for a very long time. And yet, it has just taken just an instant, for time does not really exist, but only in the physical realm.

There is so much knowledge that we wish to share with you, and our excitement rises as the time has arrived for us to do exactly that. This knowledge will be forthcoming to each and every one of you in a form that you can understand. Slowly, gently, it will be provided to you. Now is the time for you to trust your intuition, for that is how it will begin. There is no possibility of failure. For only love and joy exist and are building every day.

Accept this gift that we have for you, as we thank you for the many gifts you have already given to us. You are brave souls to have embarked upon this physical journey. For the physical state dulls the remembrance of connection. But each and every one of you came to this physical plane with a purpose in mind. And we have no doubt that you will fulfill that purpose as you move through this earthly life.

You have a foot in both worlds, and that will begin to be more obvious to you as the changes progress. Call on us for help in adjusting to this change, should you need it. You must call on us, for we cannot help without your permission. And know that we are always standing in the ready, behind you, in front of you and beside you. Every moment of your day.

> Blessings to you, Dear One,
> For embarking upon this journey.
> Accept our gifts to you,
> For you are worthy,
> And you are very much loved by the All.

Week 42

Why Not Today?

The time is right now, in this very moment,
For you to begin your new way of being.
It is a very simple process, this new beginning.
No preparation required. Just begin.
Begin to be the sacred vessel of light and love
Who casts a positive light on your surroundings.

And how do you do this? Begin with a smile. Allow yourself to feel the love that surrounds you at this very moment. Every breath draws in love. Every exhale sends out love. Peaceful existence in, loving attention out. Joyous remembrance in, warmth and compassion out.

You are a conduit for love. It flows through you and outward. Can you feel the peace settling into your being as you read these words? They are words of truth, and somewhere deep within, you remember, and the smile begins to form without effort. You feel the connection with the Mother, as your feet become one with her. The peace that you feel is calming and familiar. You are grounded, you are connected and you are one.

And in this moment, in this state of being, your mind is clear. No worries, no schedules, no judgment. This is your reservoir of strength, that is present at all times. This is how you begin. Today. What comes next is a moment of insight, a spark of remembrance, a release of tension. Allow it, embrace it and understand that this is the beginning.

For the next few moments, close your eyes and practice this exercise, and we shall guide you down your path. Gently, lovingly and always by your side.

Breathe in.
Breathe out.
Smile and feel the love surrounding you.
And when you finish,
Give gratitude for all that you have,
For all that you are.

Why not begin today?

Week 43

Opportunity and Abundance

Every moment presents
An opportunity for change,
An opportunity for love,
An opportunity for true vision,
Every moment of your day.

How often do you take those endless opportunities to make a difference in your life? Many see their daily lives as lives of repetition and drudgery. The same thing every day. They are bored. They feel hopeless. They ask *Is this all there is in life?*

And yet, *you* have the power every moment of your day to change. Not just one chance in a lifetime, but every breathing moment. And seizing those opportunities will energize you. They will crack open the heavy veil which may have cloaked your existence. You were not meant to do the same thing day in and day out. You are here to learn, to gain knowledge, to expand your horizons.

And this can be done in the simplest of ways. You might start by taking a different route home from your daily outing. You might start by changing your routine in the morning as you start your day, or in the evening as you prepare for rest.

Why do we encourage this practice? The human condition easily falls into a daily routine, so repetitious that you need not even focus on what you are doing. It is habit. It is familiar. This allows you more time to be *in your head* with less need to focus on your surroundings. Ego rules because you are not present in the moment. You are thinking of the past, the future.

How often have you driven to your destination and wondered how you arrived, because you were far away, lost in your thoughts? This is one reason why it is not a practice for many to be present in the moment, for you have created a condition where you do not need to be present. You are not really living your life. You are just robotically going through the motions.

And so, we encourage you to change your routine, if only slightly, every day. We understand that many of the same things need to be completed every day. But do they need to be completed in the same way, with the same attitude every day? Making even these small changes will open you up to new opportunities, because you are more present in the moment. You need to be, as you are making a change. Opportunities abound, abundance surrounds you. But it is up to you to seize them. That is your free will choice.

And as you begin to shed that cloak of familiarity, you will become more aware of those intuitive moments. Why? Because you are more engaged in your daily existence. As you face the unfamiliar, you are more apt to follow your gut feeling, your intuition. You will feel more alive. You will be more interactive with your surroundings. You will begin to notice all the beauty that surrounds you, as you awaken to the hundreds of possibilities present in every moment of your life.

Make a change. See your life from a different vantage point. You may be surprised at what you have been missing. Take a chance on life, if only a small one. The time is now to begin to break those mindless habits of existence, to which you have become so accustomed to living.

> Open your eyes,
> Open your hearts,
> Open your world
> To the abundance that surrounds you.
> It only takes a moment,
> And the opportunities are endless.

Week 44

Trust

How often have you experienced self-doubt?
How often have you questioned
The choices that you have made?
How often have you wondered
If what you heard or thought or felt is really true?

It is time to lay aside all of these feelings of self-doubt and uncertainty. The time is now to move forward with trust in your heart for how your life is unfolding. If you have moved through your life with pure intent, that is all that is needed. If you have not, but are reading these words, then it is time to accept the lessons from the past and move forward with your new-found knowledge. Do not waste time and energy chastising, worrying, going down the path of *what-if*. Trust that you are exactly where you should be in this very moment. Trust in the perfection of your world.

You are a sentient being with feelings, connections and more power than you realize. Perhaps you have used these aspects of your make-up for self-gain. Perhaps you are the one who has given your power freely to another. Or perhaps you are someone who is frozen with fear to take the next step down your path to wholeness and love.

What happened in the past no longer exists. But the lessons and knowledge gained from your past live with you still. They also reside in us, as we grow closer to understanding how best we can help and communicate with you in your daily life. For us, it is finding the way to speak to you through the human condition, so that you are able to open your heart to who you really are.

There is no concern interacting with you on a soul level, for that connection is strong and true. The challenge for us is to first appeal to that part of you that goes through the daily routine, still unsteady and uncertain of the connections you have, of where you fit into the world. All that is needed for us is a tiny crack in that human shield to allow the light to shine through.

The lessons that you learned may have felt insurmountable for you. But you are still here. You are reading these words and for us, that is the chance to share our love and knowledge with you. There is perfection in your life every day, and you are moving forward every day. The *mistakes* of old are just tools for you to use as you move forward on your path. Remember them and grow from them, as we have.

Do not put more energy into blame and regret. As we have said before, your lessons are not only for you, but for many others whom you touch every day. They also contribute to the collective consciousness. They have a purpose. That is not to say that you do not take responsibility for those actions; for you must do that in order to move forward.

If you are having difficulties releasing memories of old, there is a simple ceremony that you can do to help yourself move forward. Write down those feelings and how you feel about those actions today. Then do one of two things. The first is to bury that piece of paper in Mother Earth to be absorbed by her imminent strength and transformed into loving energy. The second is to burn that piece of paper and allow the smoke from it to rise into the ethers, to be carried away by the winds of change and forgiveness. Whichever manner you choose, include forgiveness and gratitude in your prayer, as you release the bindings of these memories. Allow yourself to be free in order to take the next step on your path back to the Source. Understand your connection to the loving Universe, of which you are an integral part.

We offer our gratitude to you for sharing those lessons with us, so that we may learn. Please understand that any forgiveness that is necessary is not needed from us. The forgiveness must come from you. Forgive yourself, forgive others and join the waves of love that are building in your world as we speak. We shudder in joyous anticipation of your awakening.

> Trust yourself and realize who you truly are
> And the integral part of life that you serve.
> You are Light.
> You are Love
> You are One.
>
> And you are never alone.

Week 45

Your Daily Interactions

How has your day been this day?
Did it go as you had planned?
Were there unexpected moments of joy
Or feelings of disappointment and frustration?

Every moment of your day is another chance to have a Divine interaction. Every moment. Even in those moments when the person with whom you are relating is unkind or negative in their attitude. *You* are the one who can change that challenging interaction into one which is holy and Divine. How do you accomplish this?

These interactions are opportunities for you to shine; to deflect the negativity and transform it into something positive and loving. For you are capable of acting in a loving manner, no matter what. The question we have for you is this – do you *act* towards others or do you *re-act* to others?

In order to move forward on your path, the choice for you to consider is to keep your power at all times. By re-acting to another's negative manner, you give away your power to them. You allow them to affect your vibration and lower it closer to where they are at the moment.

Can you instead, hold steady that power which is yours and not allow the interaction to affect you in a negative way? Can you instead, surround yourself in light and love and allow that positive energy to flow through you and into the room? Can you instead, be an example of how to interact in a gentle, kind and positive way? That is not to say that if you are in physical danger, that you do not remove yourself immediately. You are still able to send loving energies from afar.

It is difficult, we understand, to move through your days tired, stressed and feeling alone. The physical existence is a challenging one, indeed. However, it is now time for you to begin to focus more on the integral connection you have with all of creation, and how that affects your day and that of others.

It is up to you to create that tiny shift in the room from negative to positive. That does not mean you are required to say something uplifting and loving, for often that is not appropriate. But what you can do, in your new-found awareness, is to surround yourself and those with whom you interact with love and positive forces.

Are you beginning to understand how the unseen forces can play an integral part in your daily life? By not re-acting, but holding yourself and others in light, you have made a shift which, like a ripple in water, will continue to move outward from that point of origin. From you.

Should someone interact with you in a negative way, do not continue to hold onto that negativity after you leave the interaction. Instead, pause and draw a deep breath. Then imagine all that negative energy that surrounds you moving down through the soles of your feet into Mother Earth. Pull down positive, loving energy from above to replace that negativity, and see how rejuvenated you feel.

You cannot avoid these negative interactions. They will occur in your life, but what you can do is to walk in light and love. If you walk into an interaction knowing it will be this way, pause prior to approaching and surround yourself with loving energy. These are powerful, unseen forces at work.

Even though something is unseen, it does not mean it is not real and powerful. The air you breathe, the sounds you hear, are unseen yet very real. Take a chance and see how this exercise can change your daily interactions. And should you be the one feeling overwhelmed and negative, the same exercise will work for you.

Remember your Source,
Who you are
And the power you have
To change your life.
Use it wisely.
Use it in love.
And change the world.

One tiny step at a time.

Week 46

Designing Your Life

Do you know what it is
You wish to do with your life?
Are you at a crossroads,
Wondering what to do?
Is it clear in your mind
The next steps you are to take?

Dear One, your life is a time to explore new avenues of being. The possibilities for you are endless – the support, ever present. What holds you back is fear and uncertainty. Can you overcome these in order to open up your wings and fly? Do you not realize that there is always a safety net underneath you, ready to catch you if you begin to falter?

The world is yours to explore and to experience. We understand the concerns you have about having enough to survive and provide for those you love. But allowing fear to hold you back is not the way to experience this gift of life here upon this plane.

How far outside of your self-limited box have you traveled? How long have you repeated the same motions day in and day out, when they no longer feed your soul? If the longing is there, it is time for you to make a move.

Do not focus on the negative possibilities, for there are an equal number of positive responses from your actions as there are negative. And anything that occurs in your life is a movement forward – a lesson, knowledge to be shared, a new experience to allow you to grow.

Do not allow yourself to stagnate because of fear of the unknown. Instead, embrace it and take a chance. You will be amazed at what you will find and experience, and you will wonder why you did not attempt this change sooner.

Do not act impulsively, but center yourself; go within and ask yourself, your higher self, how to proceed. There is always a way. Allow the possibilities to flow within, and do not allow that analytical mind of yours to engage. Instead, open your heart to what your soul requires for the next chapter in your journey.

The veil is thinning, the rules are changing, and the possibilities are endless. It is time for you to trust your longings that need to be fulfilled. As long as you act with pure intent and not from anger or retribution or judgment, your life will unfold in a burst of color and delight. Trust.

It is time to listen to your heart, not your mind, your Ego. Manifest in your mind what it is that you want. Do this with love, and watch it begin to unfold before your very eyes. All things are possible, but it is up to you to take the first step.

Remember that you are surrounded by love. You have a squad of cheerleaders urging you on. Be honest with yourself about how you feel in your current situation. Give yourself some quiet contemplative time to connect with your higher self, and design the next step in this journey of your life.

The end result may not be exactly as you had planned, but it will allow an opportunity for you to grow, to shine, to share your gifts with others. It will allow the opportunity for you to remove yourself from a situation that no longer serves you. And in making that change, remember that you are leaving behind opportunities for others to grow in your absence.

Act in love. Believe in yourself and all the opportunities that lie ahead for you. Anticipate with joy, and take that next step with strength and resolve, knowing that you are *never* alone. Ask for help if you are feeling unsteady. There will always be strong arms around you to support you if you stumble.

Take that chance.
It is your time to shine.

Week 47

Transformation

Can you feel the pulse of change
Within your being?
Can you trust that all will unfold
Exactly as it should?
Will you accept the coming changes in your life
With grace?

Your life is not static but ever-changing. That is the design of the human existence. You are here to learn, to discover, to love, to laugh, to enjoy the beauty of the world around you. You are here to explore all the possibilities available to you. Can you go back to the child-like delight of self-discovery and step on the path of change and transformation?

Understand that your purpose for life here is to experience as much as you can. Every interaction that you have is a stepping off point for change, be it subtle change or expansive change in your life. Every moment of your life grants you the opportunity for a new discovery, a new way of being, a chance for joy and love. Every moment.

Consider changing your perspective on your life. At the end of every day, give yourself a few moments to review your day, without judgment, but only as an observer. Consider the connection that you have with each and every person with whom you interacted that day. Remember that you are One with All, and so in a sense, you interact with yourself in all situations.

What if…What if everyone took the time at the end of their day to review and to bless every interaction they had, regardless of how it went, good or bad? What if those combined blessings transformed the past and opened up the possibility for a lighter, more joyful, loving interaction the next time you meet? Remember that the moment is *now*. Offer gratitude for the lessons of the past, bless those with whom you interacted and see in your mind's eye, only gentle loving interactions in the future.

Your transformation has begun. You are ready to help change the world, and it begins with you. Can you combine all the teachings already provided into your daily life? Deep breaths, loving breaths, wrapped in light and love, walking in higher vibration, sending fear down into Mother Earth, living in the moment of *now*. If you do, you will find yourself standing taller, feeling stronger, accepting the love around you and returning it into the ethers surrounding you.

Do not allow yourself to don that victim persona, for you are not a victim of anyone or anything but your own fear. Understand the power which runs through your veins at all times. Know that when you ask for help, it is there immediately, and that the answers to your questions may come in any shape or form.

Allow the synchronicity of life to move you forward. Get out of your head and be aware of your surroundings. Instead of bullies and brutes, you will see other wounded souls like yourself, who are in need of loving kindness.

Know, truly know, that you are the writer of your own story. You can choose to put a positive or negative spin on it. Allow yourself the setbacks that you will have, for they still contribute to your forward movement along your path. Nurture yourself as you would a child who needs a loving embrace. You are on your way. Your transformation has begun. You are worthy, and you are loved, and you are a powerful force of light and love.

Ah, what wonders of life lay before you. Open your eyes to the beauty and love that surround you, and see the reflection of light and love staring back at you when you look into a mirror.

Your beacon of light shines brightly;
The embers within are ready
To burst forth into a steady flame.
Your transformation has begun.

And we sing with joy for its coming!

Week 48

What Does the Future Hold?

Do you worry about tomorrow?
Is it coming too quickly
Or perhaps not quickly enough?
Will you be ready
For the changes that are coming?

Be joyful of the many opportunities and possibilities that present themselves to you every moment in your life. They are there, right in front of you. Just push that curtain of fear aside, and you will see them, like pieces of candy to be plucked and savored.

Move forward in your life with joy and anticipation, not with dread or worry. Remember that you can see your future in either a positive or negative way. Banish that fear, and allow the buzz of excitement to fill your ears, for all the possibilities being laid at your feet. So many choices, all placed at the beginning of a different path back to the Source. For remember that all paths lead back to the Source. All paths.

Take a deep breath and allow yourself to dream. Dream big. Dream goodness and joy. Dream love and peace and gentle movement forward. Remember that you have a purpose here upon this earthly plane, and you will be gently nudged forward to fulfill that purpose. No purpose is too small. No purpose is so large that it is impossible to do. Each and every one of you has a unique gift, a special niche, a perfect placement to fulfill your purpose here upon this plane.

Trust. Be aware of how your life flows, and if you require guidance, just ask. Ask for clarity, ask for help. Ask for the ability to see the opportunities that lay before you. Then dig down deep within yourself, and pull up that courage that is sitting there in repose. There is plenty there for you to use as needed, as you move forward. And remember that every step you take is forward movement. *Every* step.

Reach out and take our hand extended to you in loving support. Understand that you have more power, more strength, more resolve than you realize. You have the knowledge of the Universe at your fingertips. It is time to skip, to dance, to embrace your life and to make any changes that you feel guided to make. We are always there right by your side, whispering encouragement in your ear, cheering you on. From our perspective, you are filled with light and love, and you leave golden drops that glisten in your wake, as you move forward every moment of your day.

Be at peace with who you are and what you are capable of doing. Whatever you think, the reality is much greater than that. You are a part of the All, and with that comes all of its knowledge and power and love. Do not doubt yourself, for we do not doubt you for a moment.

Dear brave soul, we thank you for your journey and for the knowledge you share with us every day. We give back to you all that we have, in ways that you as an individual can accept. Each and every one of you is a beacon of light, shining brightly.

> You are Strength.
> You are Power.
> You are Knowledge,
> You are Wisdom.
>
> You are Joy.
> You are Peace.
> You are Love Incarnate.

Week 49

Transitions are Occurring

The energies are raising here
Upon this earthly plane.
This has been a long time coming
And we rejoice in its occurrence,
Here and now.
The time has come for all
To begin their transitions
Within this earthly plane.
For each and every one of you,
This will manifest a different way.

You are all connected, not only to this earthly plane but to the heavenly vistas above and around you. What is occurring at this point of time is a thinning of the veils that separate these two dimensions. For many of you, this will not require any changes for you or affect you in any major way.

But for others, you will see, feel and experience physical, mental and emotional changes in your daily life. For you, we give our encouragement, our focus and our help as you ask for it. And now is a time to ask for that help. There is no need for concern, but there is a need for action. Call on us to guide you as to what action is needed for you individually. It is all a matter of readjusting your thoughts, your words, your deeds and how you walk through your daily life.

For those of you who are feeling these effects, understand that your way of living must change to allow your light to shine – for your path to widen and clear, in order for you to move forward. There is nothing to fear, there is no judgment, no punishment, no reason to worry about ramifications from your actions past, present or future. This life of yours is beginning to expand, and each of you who are beginning to feel the effects of this expansion must allow room in your life for this expansion to occur and continue.

You, you are the vehicle, the vessel of change. You are the one who has committed to partake in these changes, that are occurring at this time. You are the one who we honor for your dedication to moving forward on your path, and while doing so, clearing the way for others to follow. You are the teacher, the star who shines brightly enough to light the way for others.

We understand that you may not feel that way at this very moment. But we know who you really are and the power you hold at your fingertips to help move things forward, as they accelerate the way of being here upon this plane.

You, you are the one who is the chosen, the leader, the seer, the visionary, the guide for those who follow behind you. Your time is now to make the changes necessary to move forward. Tend your physical body, for it is the vessel given to you to house your very soul.

Do not doubt that the vessel you are using has not been purposefully selected for the tasks you are meant to do. Do not doubt that you are or will be placed in the perfect location to do your work, that which calls to you. Heed that call. It is no longer possible for you to ignore it. Your time is now, Dear One.

Trust yourself, your purpose, your gifts, and your placement. Trust your connection and the messages that each and every one of you receives. No comparison, no judgment. Only connection, support, love and light. Call upon us. Call upon each other.

And bask in the knowledge that this is only a brief time of transition, before the skies open for you with all their glory and knowledge.

But you must be ready. You must be in order. Take the time now to prepare. And call upon us for help.

> For we understand,
> We love and honor you
> For all that you do.

Week 50

Light

The light shines upon you
And through you.
The light shines from you.
The light is building
And spreading across the world.
Across the entirety of being.

For you and for the entire Universe, this is a time of joy and celebration. Can you feel the energies rising around you? Do you notice a difference in the air? Even if you do not yet feel these changes, they are here and you will benefit from them in ways you have not envisioned.

Be of joy, no matter what you perceive as positive or negative in your daily life. Be of joy. For you are part of the continuum which is shifting, changing, expanding, and these changes include you in your daily life. Perhaps you cannot feel or see these changes, but they will affect you in a very positive way.

We have talked of the connection of the All many times. Consider then how the building of energies enhanced by light workers throughout your world and the entire continuum will also carry you along, until you are in a place, a position, to accept these changes and consciously join them. This work being done is a work of love and commitment by others who join in the vision of growth and knowledge for All.

Even if you do not understand, open your heart to the possibilities, the new opportunities that await you in your daily life. Should you have a flash of insight about something with which you have struggled, listen to it. Should you feel a strong urge to take a new path, then trust that urge and begin to follow it. There are no wrong decisions, no wrong paths if they are made, if they are taken, with pure intent, trust and love. The possibilities for you are endless.

No longer box yourself into a confined way of being. Break out of that way of being, open your mind, your heart. Share your gift with the world. And no longer say that you do not have a gift, for certainly you do. No longer can you hide that part of yourself from others, for the time is now to accept it and share it with the world.

Unbeknownst to you, the light, the energy that pulses from you and through you is changing. It must do so in order to join the expansion occurring at this moment in the Universe. Rejoice in it. Recognize those in your life who have offered their love and service to you, often just in a passing moment.

Understand that you are being lifted by others, as you read these words – by those who are aware, who love you unconditionally, even without knowing you well or even at all. And yet, they are connected with you and include you in their thoughts and prayers, in their daily intentions of light work. Understand that you are surrounded by light and love. And it is growing, becoming brighter every day.

Give gratitude to these souls who are in front of you on the path and extend to you their hands, their hearts, to help you move forward. This is not a race. There are only winners, and all are moving forward en masse. A flow of humanity. A flow of light. A movement of love spiraling around you and through you.

Blessings to all of you. We honor the work that has been done and continues to be done. We shall continue to guide all of you on this journey of light and love. We will encourage you to allow the heavy cloak of uncertainty to fall, so that you may spread your wings and begin to fly.

All is well with you.
All is well within the Universe.
All is filled with light and with love.
Be at one with it.
Accept your place
In this joyous celebration.

For you *are* very much a part of it.

Week 51

The Joy of Being

Can you be at one
With the beauty that surrounds you?
Can you allow the light to shine
Within and around you?

Your essence, your very essence, consists of light. That light is
embodied in your physical vessel to move and exist here upon this
physical plane. It is a temporary existence here, for your natural state
of being is in another dimension. And a part of you still exists there
as well, while part of you discovers yourself on this plane.

The purpose of your being here is to explore, to discover, to expand
your knowledge, and to shine your light as a beacon for others. Being
enveloped in a physical vessel is difficult, we understand, for you are
more familiar with a lightness of being, a freedom of movement,
unlimited by the heaviness of the physical form.

But please understand that this journey, this adventure of which you
are partaking, is one chosen by you at a time prior to your birth here.
And when that choice was made, it was made with love and joy and
excitement for learning, growing and sharing the experiences from
this plane.

This dis-connection that you might feel is only an illusion. For you
are connected and have always been connected, to a part of yourself
outside this physical plane, as well as to the continuum that exists
into infinity. Reach down deep within yourself in moments of quiet,
and find that connection that has always been there. See it as a
cord of light, glistening, pulsing with a brightness beyond anything
possible on this physical dimension.

You, you are a piece of all of this. You are that light, and with that light comes a joy beyond measure. With that light comes a connection that is strong, that is steady and unbreakable. This is who you truly are. You are *not* a physical body, just as you are not the garments that you place upon this physical frame. You are much more than that. You are power and you are strength. You are wisdom and you are knowledge. You are an integral piece of the All, who was courageous enough to come here to learn, to experience an existence different from any which you had previously.

Not all chose to come here. But you did with a hunger for new experiences. You made the decision with lightness in your heart and joy in the anticipation of new possibilities of life. You must understand the joy that was felt when this decision was made, and you must understand the joy that will surround you upon your return. This is your chosen journey, and we are here with you, but in another dimension, another plane that exists exactly in the same space, but at a higher vibration. So you are within an arm's reach of us, always.

Understand the joy of being that this existence brings not only to us, but to another part of you who still remains with us on this dimension. This part of you is your higher self, who vibrates at a higher frequency and guides you as you navigate your daily physical life. Your higher self anchors you to your natural state of being, as you experience your adventures here upon this physical plane. That pulse of light, that connection is to a part of you who sits with us as we guide you and send you our love, every moment of your day.

Accept these truths in your heart, if you are able. And if it appears too outrageous, then just consider that what we say here is a possibility. If nothing else, accept our love for you. Call upon us for help in a whisper, in a shout, in a prayer. It matters not, for we always hear you. How can we not, when we are here right next to you, always.

You are a Joy of Creation.
You are Light.
You are Love.

And you are loved, unconditionally.

Week 52

One

Can you feel the connection?
Can you trust the connection?
Can you use the connection
To move forward in your world?

One. That is all there is, only One. And you are very much an integral part of this Oneness, like a cell in your physical body that works in conjunction with all the other cells, to create a functioning, complete entity. All of these cells join together to allow the physical body to move, to exist and to create. Alone, one cell can do nothing. But when connected to the entirety, it allows the body to move forward, to function in the physical world.

And so, you, the *real* you, is connected to the Oneness, which could not exist without your input, without the part that you play to help It to move forward. There have been many names, many descriptions of this totality of being, and we shall not argue with any of those. For each and every one of you, the connection has a slightly different meaning, a different purpose in your life, and so you each have a different description that you use.

All of that matters not. What matters is how you use that connection and how you contribute to the growth and knowledge of the All. Do you walk with pure intent, non-judgment and lightness of being? Or do you pounce on anyone who does not share your personal beliefs? Do you close yourself off to any differences from your personal way of living? Have you closed down your mind, your life, to the infinite possibilities of new experiences?

These new experiences can occur in a moment, by being more aware of your surroundings and noticing anew something that has been there all along. You might suddenly notice the fear, the hesitation, in the voice of someone to whom you have readily given your power. Or you may suddenly realize the strength that flows within the veins of someone you barely noticed in the past. The possibilities are endless, of the knowledge that is waiting for you to pluck from the everyday moments of your life.

Open your eyes, your ears, your heart to your daily life and see, hear and feel what you have been missing. Just be aware, take in that information, sit with it and see where it takes you, how it will change your way of being, if ever so slightly. For it will and it does every day, often un-noticed by you, because you are in your head, playing the same song over and over, while at the same time, a new symphony is offering you a new way of being.

You, you are the eyes, the ears, the heart of the Oneness. You are like the Voyager craft that is now seeking new information outside of your solar system. You are the seeker, the information gatherer, the courageous adventurer. Separate, but connected. An individual, yet part of the All. Both collector and giver of knowledge, every moment of your day.

Be at peace with who you are and with your place in the Universe. Your life is not only in this world, but expands far beyond. Begin to think bigger, dream larger, reach further than you ever have before. The possibilities, the opportunities are endless. For you are a part of the whole, the One, the All. And your life here, now, is precious and meaningful. Beyond your comprehension.

> You are Power.
> You are Strength.
> You are Knowledge.
> You are Wisdom.
> You are Light and you are Love.
>
> Always and forever more.

A Final Message

To close, a personal message from the scribe.

At times of personal or worldly stress, I have a personal mantra I use that helps me find balance once again, and perhaps it will help some of you. Change the words as needed, and allow it to flow freely from your heart.

I thank you all for reading this book and for the light each and every one of you sends out into the world. Please continue to do so, as it is greatly needed at this time. Never forget that you *are* Light and Love and are always surrounded by it, no matter how dire you feel.

May you know peace and joy always.

My Mantra

I am Peace.
I am Love.
I am Light.
I am One.

I am Joy.
I am Laughter.
I am Grace.
I am Love.
I am One.

I am Knowledge.
I am Power.
I am Wisdom.
I am Strength.
I am Love.
I am One.

I am Balance.
I am Creativity.
I am Connection.
I am Truth.
I am Light.
I am Love.
I am One.

I am Free.

Reader's Guide

Personal growth is not done in a day, a week or even a year. It takes time and involves meditation, reflection and honesty, as you begin the process of healing. Throughout this book, you have been encouraged to move forward and to begin to shed old ways of being, discarding judgment and fear. I've added some questions below, which may help you as you continue on your journey of self-discovery.

These questions could be discussed in a group setting or alone, in quiet reflection. Journaling would be helpful as you start to peel back the layers of your life and allow your inner light to shine. Be gentle with yourself as you go through this process. Remember that your purpose for being here is to learn, and in that process, we all stumble along the way.

1. **Week Three states that fear is present in all aspects of your life.**
   Can you review your life and observe how you have given fear power? How can you remove this fear from your life?

2. **Throughout this book, there is mention of a web of connection with all things.**
   How do you envision that and how do you think that affects your life? Does it make you feel less alone, more empowered?

3. **Week Ten talks about how kindness is often perceived as being weak, when in fact it requires much strength and courage.**
   Can you think of times in your life when acts of kindness by you or directed towards you showed strength and courage?

4. **Week Eleven talks about reclaiming your power.**

    What ways have you given away your power to others?
    How are you not using your personal power in your life?
    How often do you re-act rather than act?

5. **Week Fifteen talks of perception and how a certain event can be seen from many different perspectives.**

    Can you choose a personal event in your life and reflect
    on the different perspectives from which it can be
    viewed? By doing so, can you find compassion for others
    who were involved in that event?

6. **There is much written about raising your vibration.**

    Can you reflect upon how living in joy and love rather
    than fear and judgment might raise your vibration? What
    are some specific ways you can raise your vibration
    through joy in your life? Do you notice a difference in
    how others respond to you when you come from joy
    rather than fear?

7. **Week Thirty-two asks if you know what you really want.**

    Can you verbalize what would make you happy today?
    Can you imagine how it would make you feel when you
    received it? Is what you want today different than what
    you wanted in the past? If so, how has that changed
    and why?

8. **Are you aware of your own intuition?**

    Can you remember times when it has helped you? How
    often do you notice this in your life, and is it occurring
    more often?

9. **Do you have a daily spiritual practice?**

    If not, what could you do for a few minutes every day to
    help you feel more connected to your Divine self?

10. **Think of how you moved through your day.**

Did you complete all the tasks you wanted to get done? If not, did you feel that you failed? How did you feel about those tasks? Did you focus on each one with joy, or did you rush through them so that you could cross them off your list?

11. **Think of the interactions you had today.**

Did you give them your full attention and listen to what the other person said? Or were you multi-tasking or already thinking of a reply while they were still talking? Did you view any of your interactions today as sacred interactions?

Acknowledgements

The further I travel on this path, the more I realize that nothing is accomplished by a single individual's effort. The web of connection that surrounds all of us lays the groundwork for insight, synchronicities and joined forces to create and develop the final outcome.

So too, with the publication of this book. From my dearest Tovarysh who have given me these words to print, to those who encouraged and supported me along the way, to those who helped with the final process of creating, editing and publication – the list is endless. I cannot take sole credit for this book, and I express my gratitude to all, seen and unseen, who helped me get to this point of publication of volume two in the OWAT series.

To my friends, who were there for me, supporting me through the challenging times and believing in me until I finally began to believe in myself...thank you.

To Laura Sarno, Terry Yuschok and all those who have supported me by providing the funding for publishing this book...thank you.

To Deborah Oster Pannell for holding my hand along the way, for her professional advice and copy editing, to Lillian Ann Slugocki for creating the template for this series and to Jennifer Dopazo for her award-winning cover design...thank you.

To all of those who read the manuscript and offered testimonials for this book...thank you.

To Balboa Press for getting the manuscript through the final process of publication and marketing...thank you.

And to all of my readers, who inspired me to keep going with their kind words of encouragement and gratitude…thank you.

This has been a joint effort, and I am humbled and grateful to have had all of you join in to make this possible. May we continue to do what we can do to share the love and change this world, one word, one breath at a time.

About the Author

Celine Koropchak has been receiving messages from her "Tovarysh" for over 30 years. She gave her divine messengers this name when she was a child and they have remained a benevolent presence in her life to this day. "Tovarysh," (pronounced, Toh-VASH), is the word for friend in the Slavic language.

A graduate from Bucknell University, Celine pursued a career in medical research both at Stanford University Medical Center and Duke University Medical Center. She has over 30 publications in scientific journals. Twelve years ago, Celine became a blueberry farmer, in addition to pursuing her professional career. Now retired, she continues to hone her farming skills, with her bushes yielding over 3000 pounds of blueberries each season.

Following the guidance of her Tovarysh to share the divine wisdom passed down to her, she started a blog five years ago, TheTovaryshConnection. Later, she assembled a collection of these messages as a practical tool for readers and published her first book, *One With All of Thee: Growing Your Sacred Connection.*

One With All of Thee: Sowing the Seeds for Change is the second book in the One With All of Thee (OWAT) series. This collection of practical wisdom continues where the first book left off, speaking directly to the challenges of a time of great change and spiritual growth. It guides us to the next level of personal development with tools designed to support us in our spiritual evolution.

Celine speaks and teaches locally in the Raleigh-Durham area. Find her on Facebook (One With All of Thee) and on Twitter (@ OneTovarysh). She can be contacted at onewithallofthee@gmail.com.

NOTES

NOTES

NOTES

Printed in the United States
By Bookmasters